TABLE OF CONT

I. FOREWORD

Today, several countries are tackling the debate on institutional reform. The issues of state structure and the protection of minorities are constantly present both in Eastern and Western European countries.

The Conference of Cividale has tried to analyze, in the framework of an adequate and current cultural, political and historical reflection, how each type of state (federal, regional or other) responds to the problems of minorities and how they can contribute to finding solutions to some fundamental questions:

- Which general or special autonomous structures allow better protection of different ethnic, religious, cultural and linguistic identities while at the same time guaranteeing the respect of democratic principles? How can unity be structured out of diversity?

- In which ways can the recognition of a certain level of regional or local autonomy and the application of the subsidiarity principle, respond to the requirements for the defence and the development of minorities?

- What role is to be attributed, in respect of minorities, to regional and local structures?

- In the analysis of state structures, how can the requirements of stable and decentralised national structures be associated to the objective of a stronger integration between European states?

- Finally, what new perspectives can the process of European integration introduce in order to resolve, in a correct and sustainable manner, the problem of minorities?

Several experts on the subject and political personalities from the 39 member countries of the Council of Europe were present at the Conference. Their interventions could represent an important contribution to the debate on the protection of minorities in Europe.

****

The Congress of Local and Regional Authorities of Europe wishes to thank Mr Eugenio Ambrosi and Mrs Paola Tabor of the Friuli-Venezia-Giulia Region for their contributions to the Italian texts.

II. INTERVENTIONS

Mrs Alessandra GUERRA,
Councillor for community affairs and external relations, education and culture of the Autonomous Region of Friuli-Venezia-Giulia, Chairman of the minorities working group of the Assembly of European Regions (AER), Member of the Congress of Local and Regional Authorities of Europe

(Greeting in Friuli) *

In the context of the work of the Regional Directorate for Community Affairs and Foreign relations, I have for some time been following with attention, through the foreign relations service, the international debate on ethnic and linguistic minorities, especially in the context of interregional linkages.

Last July, in the Regional and Cultural Directorate, a minority language service was set up, responsible for administering regional legislation on protection and development of the Slovenian and Friuli languages and culture, which, it is anticipated, will also be involved in safeguarding other minority and regional cultures and languages found in the region.

Through these two bodies, therefore, the Regional Council is undertaking a series of initiatives which, taken together, make it quite clear why the Friuli-Venezia-Giulia Region decided to organize this Conference in collaboration with the Council of Europe.

Let us look first at the international context. In this respect it should be noted that only yesterday, in the Cividale Council Chamber, two working groups met which the Regional Administration is watching with particular interest and attention: the minorities working groups of the Association of the Eastern Alps (Alpe-Adria) and of the Assembly of European Regions.

The Alpe-Adria Minorities Working Group, which has now been active in the Cultural Commission of this Association for more than ten years, is currently coordinated by Somogy in Hungary. In the Alpe Adria framework, where the presence of minorities is a reflection of the wealth and complexity of situations which have probably no equal in Europe, these issues have been the subject of specific and careful study almost since the birth of the Association in 1978, and among the other activities, I would like to recall the holding in October 1993 in Bled, with some eighty participants, of a study seminar on minorities in the Alpe Adria area, the reports of which were published in December 1994.

The Working Group is continuing its work and today intends to set up an observatory for minority problems in the area and to revise the analytical study on minorities previously published in 1988, so as to take into account the expansion of the Association to include Hungarian Committees,

---

* After a brief greeting in Friuli, the Councillor gave her address based on the notes which are reproduced here in the original text, unrevised by the Author.

which were then still excluded from Alpe-Adria, and the new Slovenian and Croatian legislation following the independence of the two republics. It is precisely down this road that yesterday the Working Group sought to make further progress.

This involves two ambitious and thus expensive initiatives which it is hoped to fund through financial support from the European Union in the context of community programmes open also to non-community countries, which, in Alpe-Adria, are Hungary, Slovenia and Croatia.

Still on the subject of Alpe-Adria, it should be noted that in the Youth Working Group, too, attention was focused on the issue of ethnic and interracial cohabitation: the Friuli-Venezia-Giulia Region itself promoted a study seminar in September 1994 in Gorizia and Nova Gorica in Slovenia on how young people in border regions live out their childhood in three societies, based on ethnic background, State and nationality. Almost a hundred young people participated in the seminar, the report of which was published in Spring 1995, and was distributed, inter alia, in high schools of the region to encourage the widest possible dissemination of the issues discussed in Gorizia. In October 1995, in Milan, in conjunction with the Lombardy Region, a study seminar was held on "diversity and immigration: mechanisms for constructing identities and differences, management of intercultural conflict, educational measures", in which the issue of the constitution of new minorities in our countries and the birth of a society increasingly characterised by encounters, confrontations and meetings between different cultures was addressed in depth.

In the context of the AER - Assembly of European Regions, our own region has often supported the value of setting up a working group specifically on minority issues, and this came about in Vitoria (Spain) on 6 October 1995 under the First Commission for Institutional Affairs and it was then ratified by the General Assembly in Anversa on the following 20 October. The Friuli-Venezia-Giulia Region was entrusted with coordinating this new working group, which before yesterday had already met in Klagenfurt, in Austria and County Hall, in England.

The working group undertook a review of international activity in the field of minorities and the preparation of a document containing the political commitment of the AER Regions to respect existing international texts (Convention for the Protection of Human Rights and Fundamental Freedoms, Vienna Declaration of Heads of State and of Government, Charter for Regional or Minority Languages, etc.), to encourage national authorities to sign and/or ratify them, if they have not already done so, and then to respect them. It is also proposed in the document that, in the context of the above-mentioned constitutional review, there should be inserted in the AER Constitution an express reference to the need to work positively in this field and it should indicate, in relation to associated bodies, a political body to which minority representatives could turn for support in their own political and institutional problems. Yesterday, the working group reported on its work up to now and on the discussions so far held on the document in the competent Commissions, and has left the way clear to the final draft of the document which will be submitted to the AER Institutional Affairs Commission and from there sent to the Political Office for insertion in the Agenda of the General Assembly in Basle in December.

It is recalled in this respect that in the past, apart from the normal work carried out by the respective Commissions I - Institutional Affairs; II - East-West Interregional Co-operation and Relations with the CSCE/OSCE - Conference/now Organization of Security and Cooperation in Europe; VI - Minority and Regional Culture and Languages, our Region through the AER Committee for Development of Relations between the regions of East and West presented an initial report in Bratislava in 1992 on Alpe-Adria minorities, which was then updated and presented in Cracow in 1994 under the auspices of the Commission for Interregional Cooperation and relations with the CSCE last March in Budapest at a Forum promoted under the West-East Parliamentary Practice Project, an initiative co-financed by the Commission of the European Community to develop an exchange of Western and Central and East European experience in democracy and participation.

In AER's own activities in the Region, also last year in Vitoria, it was proposed to hold the present conference in collaboration with the Council of Europe. The Region is no stranger to collaboration with the Council of Europe, which in October 1994 promoted the 6th Conference of European Border Regions in Lubliana and on that occasion as President of the Regional Council I was included in the official speakers to give a report on the experience of the Autonomous Region of Friuli-Venezia-Giulia on minorities in the specific sectors of culture and education.

Also in the context of the Association of European Border Regions (AEBR) our region presented in Castoria, Greece, in 1993, a full report on the Association of the Eastern Alps (Alpe-Adria) focusing in particular on the legal aspects of the importance of peaceful co-existence in the Eastern Alps between diverse ethnic groups and cultures, as an instrument of development of communities which live along the borders. In view of the importance of this issue along all Europe's borders, AEBR, which no more than a month ago in Gorizia held a meeting of its own Executive Committee, expressed interest in our initiative and is here today with its senior officials, and we look for a positive impact of today's initiative and more generally in our activity within AEBR itself.

I would like to recall once more the concrete possibility of using a new and important instrument, the one offered to our communities by the Community Interreg 2 Programme and the Cross Border Programme, the first to make use of structural funds for regions within countries of the EU and the second using PHARE funds for European regions in countries outside the Community.

Under these programmes, perhaps for the first time, it is possible to undertake concrete actions relevant to the realities of the borders of Friuli-Venezia-Giulia, Carinthia and Slovenia and soon in Croatia through specific measures on matters of concern to the minorities present there: cultural, scientific, economic, awareness and development, aimed at overcoming old suspicions and hostilities which are still harboured by our people and to create the foundations for greater confidence in cohabitation. In aiming at greater confidence in civil and institutional co-existence, for example, there should be a study of the possibility of using the Interreg Fund to carry out a major research, on social, economic, cultural and legal premises, into the feasibility of a Euroregion of the Friuli-Venezia-Giulia, Carinthia, Slovenia triangle, which could serve as a springboard for the proposal, for the first time in more than a hundred years of the modern Olympiad, to hold within our borders the 2006 Winter Games "sans frontières."

Allied to this intense activity in the international context, similar attention has been devoted in recent years to the internal situation in our regional territory, characterised by the presence of more ethnic and linguistic minorities.

The authority to deal with this complex and fascinating subject derives from the Statute giving Autonomy to the Friuli-Venezia-Giulia Region which in article 3 recognizes the equal rights and equal treatment of all citizens, regardless of the linguistic group to which they belong.

It is emphasized that, apart from this rule of principle there are no special attributions of regional powers, unlike other Regions with Special Statues which in the Constitution and successive implementing legislation have powers in this area, for example, the education sector (nursery schools and compulsory schooling). However, specifically, the education sector in Friuli-Venezia-Giulia remains under the State legislation which, on education, guarantees the use of the language and representation in the school of the Slovenian minority, but does not take account of other minority languages or minorities.

11

Bearing in mind that the Friuli-Venezia-Giulia Region regards the protection of regional and minority cultures as an issue central to development of the special autonomy and regional and minority cultures as essential elements in the ethnic and historical identity of the regional community (as recently set out in regional law L.R.15/1996) since the 80s, parallel to developments at national level, regional legislation has grown up, mainly in relation to cultural activities, reflecting the pluricultural reality and the many cultural and linguistic entities just within the borders of the regional territory.

As early as the first survey by the Association of the Eastern Alps, at the end of the 1980s, it was noted that in the Friuli-Venezia-Giulia Region, apart from the Slovenian minority, the Friuli group, the Veneto group and the German community and the region itself were also regarded as one of the foremost regions of Italy in respect of the extent of the use of the mother tongue.

As far as the region is concerned, the first significant intervention was L.R. 68/1981, which, in Title VI, provided for contribution aid to support "activities intended to protect and promote the Friulian language and culture and other local cultures and languages", identifying, in addition to the Friulian language, language and culture of Slovenian, German and Venetian origin.

There was a change in the law with the State law 19/1991 which provided, in relation to border areas, an "ad hoc" budget to support cultural and artistic initiatives in favour of the Slovenian minority in Italy "pending approval of an organic law to protect the Slovenian minority" itself.

While, with respect to the State, we are still awaiting the above-mentioned protection law, the region has operated on the premise of that law with its own regional law, 46/1991 as subsequently amended, consolidating in a single text the existing legislation in various areas of competence for the Slovenian minority which had previously been financed (press, culture, theatre, cultural exchanges, support for educational institutions, recreational activities, choirs and folklore), thus bringing about a specific regional legislation.

At this point, it is to state the obvious to highlight that the financial support obtained so far has been crucial to the very survival of these cultural, scientific and scholastic institutions for the Slovenian minority in the region, as the connecting fabric, as is already apparent, moreover, in the constitution of the Friuli-Venezia-Giulia region.

The region will thus be the voice of these institutions in order to ensure that the work to already undertaken by these institutions, with contributions from State funds, protection and promotion of the cultural, ethnic and linguistic heritage of the Slovenian minority which belongs to all the Friuli-Venezia-Giulia Region, is not prejudiced.

In the 1980s and 90s, and following the tragic events which struck Friuli with the 1976 earthquake, there has been a new desire for linguistic and cultural identity by the people of Friuli, who form a majority in Friuli-Venezia-Giulia and are present in most of the Association (as recently shown also by communes in Udine, Pordenone and Gorizia).

Through regional Laws L.R. 6/1992 and 48/1993, there has been a significant change in relation to Friulian culture, when that year, for the first time the region legislated for global protection of the Friulian language and culture, also setting up a "Scientific observatory of language and culture" which has begun its work in the last few months and can be expected to make a significant contribution to the establishment of an "Observatory of the minorities" in the Association of the Eastern Alps.

The requirement for a global approach to measures concerning regional and minority languages, just this year, has led the regional Administration to make specific administrative provision, the above-mentionned "Regional and minority language service" which will be have the task, apart from undertaking measures in this sector which were previously uncoordinated, of introducing rules on minority and regional languages and culture which up to now have not been subject to specific and focused measures, such as the German, Venetian and Ladin language and culture.

At a time when the debate on minorities in Europe is a concern of so many States, either with regard to institutional reform or legislation in favour of minorities, the Friuli-Venezia-Giulia region, which, as we should recall, is one of the most interesting in its use of so many languages, can play an important role in developing its own special autonomy, regarding the protection of regional and minority cultures as an essential and core issue.

Mr Leon KIERES,
Vice-President of the Congress of Local and Regional Authorities of Europe

Mr Chairman, Ladies, Gentlemen and Colleagues,

I have pleasure in welcoming you to this conference on behalf of Congress of Local and Regional Authorities. I believe that such international meetings and discussions at our Conference help towards a better mutual understanding between participants from different countries.

Our present Conference on federalism, regionalism, local autonomy and minorities, which I now have the honour to open, which is undoubtedly an important event, is the truly international meeting of political personalities and experts on the subject of protection of the rights of minorities.

Why the problem of minorities is so important? Why international communities should deal with it? Unfortunately, as last years events and experiences have shown us, the minorities problems are not internal matters of states. The destruction of former Yugoslavia is a meaningful example.

Minority in relation to majority may be sometimes an endangering factor. But minorities should be acknowledged as a factor which enrich the science and culture without obliteration of their ethnic identity.

The uniformity is not possible without diversity. The variety of cultures and customs creates a firm foundation for the state. Lack of tolerance for aspirations of national minorities causes wars and conflicts. Tolerance is the basis of state stability. As results from history, depreciation of minorities aspirations means neglecting of the history of the country.

On the other hand, minorities should take into consideration economic potential of the state. Minority should not be especially privileged in any case.

Sometimes, there were raised objections to international community about interference in internal affairs of state concerning minority. In fact, the interference is unadvisable, but much desirable is exchanging of experiences, sharing of methods and ways of solving minority problems, sometimes well known since centuries.

I would like to recall that the Council of Europe has drawn up instruments of international law dealing with the protection of minorities and their languages, namely the Framework Convention for the protection of national minorities and the European Charter for regional or minority languages. Representatives of the states in the Congress are asked to urge their respective governments to sign and ratify these two texts. The accession to the European Charter for regional or minority languages entails specific undertakings with regard to the linguistic rights of members of minorities.

At the Vienna Summit in October 1993, making life better for minorities was named as one of the Council of Europe's main aims in the years ahead. This policy was rapidly reflected in the 1994 Framework Convention for the Protection of National Minorities, signed so far by thirty-two of the thirty-nine member States and ratified by Romania, Hungary, Slovakia and Spain. But the Council also saw the need for practical, on-the-spot action - which is where its programme of "confidence-building measures" with technical and financial aid for projects aimed at fostering good community relations comes in. The first confidence-building measures for the former Yugoslavia were introduced in 1994 as part of the local democracy embassies scheme launched by the Congress of Local and Regional

15

Authorities. Examples include the civil society school at Osijek (Western Slavonia) and the inter-regional television station at Maribor (Slovenia) both of which got financial backing. Another is the inter-ethnic "peace school" at Gorski Katar in Croatia.

I should like to say that the Congress of Local and Regional Authorities of Europe, since the very beginning, have taken a positive attitude with regard to the problem of protecting minorities. Congress have always supported this activity and it shall continue to support it in the future.

The Congress firmly believes that the cultural policy of local and regional authorities is an important element, enabling citizens to become aware of their regional identity as they develop roots in an environment on a human scale and take on active responsibility for participating in the different self-governing administrative bodies.

The Congress encourages the competent local and regional authorities to initiate cultural programmes, geared to young people in particular, with a view to raising awareness of the idea of cultural diversity which constitutes a most valuable part of European heritage. The knowledge of this diversity contributes to the creation of a spirit of tolerance and solidarity.

The Congress also condemns all declarations or interference attempts aiming at a solution of ethnic minority problems by the use of force.

One of the most important areas of CLRAE activity is democracy for peace, which comprises, among others, above mentioned local democracy embassies. Three years ago CLRAE introduced local democracy embassies. These embassies, which are on the territory of the former Yugoslavia, are a Congress innovation and allow us to perform a preventive role wherever there is a risk of conflict. The idea is an outstanding one. The Congress was right to involve a number of municipalities and regions in operating them but CLRAE is not going to leave the embassies to their own devices. CLRAE is having a duty to monitor their work and make sure they are staying faithful to the original concept. To that end CLRAE is going to improve their functioning despite the problems of financing the local democracy embassies.

In this connection it also seems that, in the new democracies, which is where people are learning to operate democratic, local and regional institutions, it would be worth having local information offices on the same lines as the local-democracy embassies.

Dear and distinguished friends, in the name of Congress of Local and Regional Authorities and in my personal capacity, I express the hope that your deliberations will prove fruitful, that they will lead to increase in our knowledge and will contribute to the successful solution of the complex problems of local autonomy and minorities.

Mr Gianfranco MARTINI,
Member of the Congress of Local and Regional Authorities of Europe (CLRAE)

Introductory Report

This introductory report, which the Council of Europe has asked me to draft, must not, I think, anticipate the reports which are to be presented during the conference. Its contents must not venture into too much technical detail, nor must it be solely concerned with workers and employees. On the contrary, this introductory report <u>should</u> offer some food for thought (to be discussed in greater depth and detail during the conference) about:

1. The reasons which prompted the joint organisers (the Congress of Local and Regional Authorities of the Council of Europe and the Friuli-Venezia-Giulia Autonomous Region) to suggest the holding of this conference, with special reference to some of the most significant precedents in the activities of the Council of Europe and its Congress of Local and Regional Authorities, in this sphere.

2. The reasons for the choice of the general theme "Federalism, Regionalism, Local Authorities and Minorities" and a brief mention of the connection between its components, especially the complex issue of minorities, and the need for autonomy and appropriate solutions, including institutional arrangements, in the relevant systems of government.

3. Not only the cultural, legal and economic implications, but also the political and moral ramifications entailed by any correct approach to the question of minorities, given that they affect both the "polis" (that is to say the community) and individual and collective behaviour.

4. The challenges which must be met by various international organisations, as regards subjects of concern and activities, when minority issues are under discussion.

5. Above all, as this event is being organised by the Council of Europe, the relationship between further foreseeable progress in the process of European integration and the vital protection and promotion of minorities' rights and concomitant safeguards, not only at national level.

I have deliberately used the conditional tense (an introductory report <u>should</u> ...) because, if we are going to keep strictly to the timetable, it will not be possible to make anything other than a few brief comments on each of these points (to which others might be added) which, if they are considered worthy of further attention, could stimulate debate.

Let me now attempt this brief exposé, which will be far from easy.

<u>Why hold this conference? Some precedents</u>

It seems unnecessary to stress that it is plain to everyone that minorities, their problems, identity and protection constitute not only one of the sources of conflict within modern society in Europe and elsewhere in the world, but also part of its potential.

The question of minorities has a direct bearing on some essential, interrelated facets of our life within the community: identity and difference; the individual and society; state, nation and citizenship; individual and collective rights; peaceful co-existence, cultural and ethnic pluralism and security.

In studies on minorities, it is always essential to bear in mind the historical dimension (events following the First World War compared with the situation today) and the political context in terms of the different régimes peculiar to various parts of western and eastern Europe.

The aforegoing already explains why the Council of Europe and on its behalf, its Congress of Local and Regional Authorities (CLRAE), focused on this topic some time ago.

A long list of positions on the subject may be found in all the studies devoted to minorities and human rights and there is therefore no need to quote them. Mention should, however, be made of the European Charter for Regional or Minority Languages, the Framework Convention for the Protection of National Minorities adopted on 10 November 1994 and opened for signature by member states on 1 February 1995, Recommendation 1201 (1993) of the Parliamentary Assembly of the Council of Europe and Resolution 232 adopted by the CLRAE in 1992 on the basis of a report I was asked to write, together with the Mayors of Budapest and Liptovsky Mikulas (representing central Europe). It heralded the organisation of this conference with a view to scrutinising local and regional schemes in Europe which are concerned with minorities, in order to see what further steps can be taken to defend them and promote their interests.

The Autonomous Region of Friuli-Venezia-Giulia, which is acting as host, is likewise worthy of attention. As it is a border region which has actual experience of the issue in its daily political, social and cultural life, we might be able to offer some useful information which could serve as a guide or yardstick.

A complicated and many-sided issue: minorities and autonomy

The title of the conference, which covers several elements and speaks volumes, reflects the CLRAE's basic frame of reference whenever it has explored the question of minorities in relation to local and regional self-government and democratic institutions, these being the sine qua non of the principle of subsidiarity and mutual trust among the various components of a complex society. At the above-mentioned plenary session of the Conference of Local and Regional Authorities (as the Congress was then called) in 1992, the theme was "Autonomy, minorities, nationalism and European Union". This conference has now taken up the subject again and is appraising it in the light of events and experiences over the last four, dramatic years, which have supplied further proof (if any were needed) that peace, democracy, respect for human rights and the ability to reconcile unity and diversity directly depend on finding the right answer to the question of minorities and to one or two other conundrums. For example, what general and specific, independent, legal and political structures are best able to protect a variety of ethnic, cultural, religious and linguistic identities while, at the same time, safeguarding the respect and promotion (and not just the passive tolerance) of human rights and the rights of peoples in the context of democracy seen as a range of values and not merely as a method or practical policy? How can the recognition of a given level of local and regional autonomy and the correct application of the principle of subsidiarity in a world viewed as a caring, global village which is willing to co-operate, provide satisfactory answers to minorities' entreaties for protection and development? What forms of government seem best suited to the achievement of this result? (It must never be forgotten that political and administrative structures do not come from the drawing-board, but are deeply influenced by the history, culture and traditions of a community.) Lastly (but I will come back to this essential point in a minute), what new prospects of a lasting solution to minorities' problems can and must the process of European unification open up by overcoming the frequent temptation to treat them purely in a national context?

As far as regional and local self-government is concerned, account must always be taken of the principles set forth in the European Charter of Local Self-Government, not forgetting the extent to which this is bound up with the cultural independence which is particularly necessary when minorities are scattered across a country. Furthermore, in what circumstances (ethnically homogeneous areas, strong sense of belonging to a minority community, linguistic and cultural traditions dissimilar to those of the majority, presence of various minority groups, etc) should minorities be allowed a suitable form of territorial autonomy (at communal, regional and intermediate level) while fully maintaining the territorial integrity of a state and loyalty to it?

What powers and territorial limits should these autonomous entities have? How to avoid the territorial independence given to minorities shutting out the national and European community and make it instead an additional spur to wider integration?

How to ensure that persons belonging to minorities are consulted when autonomy is granted, extended or altered? When a territorial unit has a population from different ethnic groups with dissimilar languages, cultures and religions, how to secure the most suitable local self-governing institutions?

These are some of the questions facing this conference.

The notion of the absolute equality of all before the law should not be interpreted to mean mere standardisation, as this is likely to lead to every intermediate institution or social group being regarded as a threat by those types of state which do not recognise any status other than that of a citizen, who may not, in that capacity, lawfully claim any right to be different or to special treatment as a member of a minority.

Of course, the protection of a minority is not automatically tied to a particular form of government (federal or unitary), but I personally believe that the federal formula provides a strong practical and theoretical base on which unity and diversity can exist side by side and pull in the same direction.

As the examples of the United States of America, Switzerland and the Federal Republic of Germany show, federalism is not bound to open the door to secession; on the contrary, it fulfils the fundamental need expressed in the words "ex pluribus unum". It therefore forms an antidote and effective alternative to the dangerous attempts to shatter the unity of a state community.

Nevertheless, the federalism in question must be genuine and not a meaningless provision of the Constitution, as events in the former Soviet Union and Yugoslavia demonstrate.

Law, politics and the cultural and national dimension of minorities' problems

Minorities pose cultural, legal and economic problems, but the nature of their difficulties is inherently political. It could not be otherwise, as they affect the fabric of the "polis", its subdivisions, the scope it affords for freedom and independence, the relationship between citizens and institutions, the application of the principle of equality before law while nevertheless respecting diversity, the sense of belonging and identity, the loyalty of the member of a community, the response of power structures to the varying aspirations of citizens and their participation in choices concerning them.

But minorities also pose moral problems to do with individual and collective behaviour and difficult choices between different priorities and which presuppose virtue (for the Greeks and in mediævil Europe, virtue was an indispensable ingredient of politics and it seems that it is once again being called for today in the comments of a number of thinkers). This virtue encompasses tolerance, prudence and consideration for others (many of the works of the philosopher Levinas, who has just died, were devoted to this subject) in dealings with people who are different and who have a culture, language, religion and traditions dissimilar to our own.

For this reason, the resolution of minorities' problems certainly necessitates debate and legal rules, but these should be buttressed by a "philosophy", a strong political will, effective institutional machinery and the long-term protection of the individual, so that they are solved not by taking a short-term view confined to the present, but by heeding values which are tied up with the future of the next generations. Furthermore, history must be remembered and attention paid to past experience, so that what Nietzsche would have called the "healing power of oblivion" and the habit of indifference to the lessons of the past do not prevail (I am thinking of conditions in Europe at the end of the First World War, but also of more recent tragedies) as the past lies at the heart of many predicaments today.

<u>International and European organisations and minorities (brief notes)</u>

The debate on minorities is being conducted at present in various institutions: the Council of Europe, the European Union and the Organisation for Security and Cooperation in Europe (OSCE).

a)   The Council of Europe is turning more and more into a think tank and a fruitful producer of legal instruments on numerous subjects, especially human rights, starting with the adoption in Rome in 1950 of the European Convention on Human Rights. Indeed it was through human rights that the Council of Europe became the first organisation to tackle the question of minorities.

Proof of the interest of the parliamentarians of the Council of Europe in this domain is to be found in successive reports: Resolution 136 (1957), Recommendation 285 (1961), Order 456 (1990), Recommendation 1134 (1990) and Recommendation 1177 (1992) in which the Assembly considered it urgent to elaborate an additional protocol to the above-mentioned convention. This was followed by Recommendation 1201 (1993) containing a draft additional protocol, as the endeavours of the Steering Committee for Human Rights (CDDH), an intergovernmental organ, had been unsuccessful in this respect.

The European Commission for Democracy through Law, the so-called "Venice Commission" was founded in 1990. It has drawn up a draft convention which tries to strike a satisfactory balance between the rights and duties of minorities and between their interests and those of states.

The last important result of the Council of Europe's activities in this field has been the Framework Convention for the Protection of National Minorities, which was adopted by the Committee of Ministers on 10 November 1994 and opened for signature by the member states on 1 February 1995.

fortunately, this framework convention makes it incumbent on contracting states to abide by its principles, but does not make such observance a right on which individuals may rely. The monitoring machinery is entirely in the hands of governments.

It is important to emphasise that even non-member states may be invited by the Committee of Ministers to accede to this legal instrument. It makes explicit reference to transfrontier co-operation, together with the right of members of national minorities to establish and maintain contacts across borders with persons lawfully staying in other states and with whom they share an ethnic, cultural, linguistic or religious identity or a cultural heritage.

b) The European Union has not drawn up any basic text on the rights of minorities, although respect for human right imbues the whole community system, viz the Treaty of Maastricht, Title I, Article F.

Nevertheless, some states which are of no mean significance within the European Union are redefining themselves in the wake of a process of demystification and, in doing so, they are re-examining national ties and hence the question of minorities.

The case law of the Court in Luxembourg has likewise incorporated the human rights safeguarded by the European Convention into the general principles of Community law. The European Parliament has concerned itself with the matter on various occasions and in its Resolution of 1994 on cultural and linguistic minorities, it expressly refers to the role of local and regional administrations.

c) The Conference on Security and Cooperation in Europe (CSCE) already included some provisions which indirectly concerned minorities in the Helsinki Final Act (1975), via the principles governing reciprocal relations between participating states.

The Madrid Meeting (1980-83) and the Vienna Meeting (1986-89) then followed. They came up with some absolutely novel texts in this sphere.

The subsequent Copenhagen document on pluralist democracy, the rule of law and the full respect of human rights was of special importance.

The Charter of Paris for a new Europe (1990) clearly confirmed previous positions. It was followed by the report of the Meeting of Experts on National Minorities in 1991, the Moscow Meeting of the Conference on the Human Dimension (1991) and the Helsinki Summit Declaration in 1992.

Nevertheless, the stance adopted by the CSCE and then by the OSCE is political and moral and has no binding or regulative force.

The CSCE has since become the Organisation for Security and cooperation in Europe (OSCE).

Legal standards are therefore needed, but do not suffice by themselves. An aphorism of Anatole France in "Le lys rouge" refers sarcastically to the "majestic equality of the law which prohibits both rich man and poor man alike from sleeping under bridges, begging in the street and stealing bread".

A neutral rule applied to people in dissimilar circumstances can have unjust consequences.

Often rules are not binding and there is no collective guarantee of the rights to which they refer. As far as minorities are concerned, another aspect is still open to debate. Is it preferable to draft specific regulations for minorities or should they be covered by the general protection of human rights - that is to say by universal provisions on the subject?. Does this novel idea imply the recognition of minorities as subjects of international law? Traditionally, only governments had this status, but has the development of international law cleared the way for new subjects, like "peoples" for example (which so far has been a sociological and not a legal term)?

What provisions on minorities have been included in the new constitutions of the countries of central and eastern Europe? What results have been achieved by the appointment of an ombudsman for minorities?

Ethno-nationalism excludes and separates through restrictive legislation on citizenship but, conversely, nationalism based on citizenship leads to forcible assimilation and levelling by integration.

It should not be forgotten that it was precisely the crucial question of the protection of minorities which led to the laying of the foundations of an international guarantee of fundamental freedoms and to the initial codification of international standards for human rights, in order to solve and also prevent conflicts.

Minorities and the unification of Europe

What connection is there between minorities and the process of European unification?

We are at present witnessing two simultaneous tendencies within European society (but which likewise exist in other parts of the world): on the one hand the quest for and discovery of a specific identity, be it ethnic, linguistic, cultural, historic or other, of particular social groups who claim the right to autonomy and self-government or, at times, independence and sovereignty, or even separation from the state within which they have lived so far.

On the other, peoples are consciously, lucidly searching for a new dimension of European togetherness, in other words, a new collective identity, able to provide them with suitable, democratic, supranational laws and institutions.

The second tendency seeks to transcend the nation-state and to create a supranational community. The desire to make Europe a genuine "common home" is linked to this tendency, albeit as yet rather vaguely. The opposite trend is typified by frequent outbursts of nationalism, the fragmentation of the existing legal and political order, expectations which minorities and peoples sometimes voice with violence in a revolt against situations which have existed for a long time, centralisation and uniformity - often imposed by force.

While in western Europe a rejection of nationalism is generally regarded as perfectly natural, in eastern Europe this conclusion cannot be taken for granted, because countries there are emerging from an ideological and political set-up in which internationalism was forced upon them. Western Europeans often find it easier to be post-nationalists. Can they understand why their counterparts in the east are, at least for the time being, post-internationalists. Moreover, in western Europe, an ethno-national revival is underway. One only has to think of the various autonomist movements which are a reaction against centralisation and a tendency towards homogenisation, or of the outbreaks of xenophobic behaviour which often spawn real racism and violence.

Against this background, it must be pointed out that an international community which is still organised on the basis of a system comprising a multiplicity of independent, sovereign states, will find it hard to solve the question of the coexistence of divers groups within states. At times, the increasing number of immigrant groups are referred to as if they were a genuine minority. To be more precise, migrant workers are not minorities in the true sense of the term because, among other things, they have foreign citizenship. But migration has become so widespread (especially in Europe) that it can no longer be overlooked and a migrants' statute may have to be contemplated, as migrants form real communities which pose a number of communication problems when local populations find themselves confronted with customs, traditions, cultures and religions somewhat different from their own. This can sometimes have dramatic consequences which take place before the eyes of the whole world.

Must we turn to the nation-state in order to contend with these challenges? Our answer is "no".

22

History shows that states do not necessarily have to be nation-states, single nation entities. The drawing of borders along ethnic dividing lines and according to ethnic criteria will frequently encounter serious obstacles and cause conflicts.

The right to an ethno-national identity exists, the right to ethno-national exclusivism does not. It lies at the root of various bad, dangerous, unacceptable practices such as forcible assimilation, the extermination of population groups and violent, enforced population exchanges between various countries.

Some state borders do not coincide with borders between national groups. In some states, the border areas are inhabited by a mixture of people with different nationalities.

The result is often a violent dispute about the scope of central government and the need to break out of the present mould in two directions: downwards, through a strengthening of regional and local autonomy and self-government, and upwards through new forms of political organisation (which are no longer identical with that of the nation-state) of a federal nature, which can foster peaceful coexistence and co-operation among different units, which freely agree to live under the same constitution.

The answer with regard to minorities, autonomy, self-determination, ethnic groups and national identities will obviously vary, depending on the kind of Europe we want: a Europe which will not go beyond the stage of a confederation of sovereign states (the traditional countries and those which might come into being if self-determination and separatism became automatic) or a Europe able to look further ahead and try out new forms of political organisation, where a difference in identity would not prevent greater solidarity and a unifying process underpinned by common institutions resting on the principle of subsidiarity.

It must be added that the former integrative effects of membership of an ethnic group should become weaker as progress is made towards multiple nationality, which will alter the psychology, feelings and actions of the new European citizen, who will have to learn to be faithful to several masters at the same time. All this should promote the peaceful coexistence of different social and cultural groups and the action of local and regional authorities can certainly provide substantial support in that direction.

In brief, the rising number of minorities in Europe is the outcome of the historic encounter between the nation-state and the diversity of the various populations with which it is abundantly endowed. This wealth of collective identities is helping to demonstrate that Europe acquires it identity solely through its diversity and that the defence of the European identity calls for the conservation of European diversity.

By inventing the nation-state, Europeans created a mechanism which produces minorities. By basing the political community on unifying factors such as religion, language and culture, the very notion of a nation created conditions making for minorities.

International protection for the identity of minorities was initially achieved through bilateral agreements: the peace treaties after the First World War and the League of Nations were no more than a temporary means of stabilising the political and territorial order after the war.

The United Nations abandoned this system in favour of the universal protection of human rights, but the limitations of its action are well known.

I strongly hope (and I believe that my feelings are shared by all the participants) that this conference will produce not only a better understanding of the complex issue of minorities and of the many and various attempts to date to find a satisfactory answer to their problems, but above all a logical political and institutional commitment at national and European level, in a context of respect for human rights and the need for autonomy, as well as for the values of genuine democracy and mutual trust, a commitment which is not just a relic of the past, but a token of faith in the prospects for a united Europe.

Mr Ferdinando ALBANESE,
Director of Environment and Local Authorities of the Council of Europe

Local and regional self-government and protection of ethnic and
linguistic minorities in the framework of the Council of Europe

I.   INTRODUCTION

1.   The Council of Europe has produced two international conventions on the question of minorities: the Framework Convention for the Protection of National Minorities and the European Charter for Regional or Minority Languages.

2.   To date (3 October 1996), the Framework Convention has been signed by twenty-eight States and ratified by five. Twelve ratifications are needed for it to enter into force. The Charter has been signed by twelve States and ratified by four. It must be ratified by five States before it enters into force.

3.   The two texts differ from three points of view: *ratione personae, ratione materiae* and with regard to the types of protection.

a)   Difference *ratione personae*

4.   The Framework Convention does not include a definition of the term "national minority" and the preparatory discussions have shown that it will be interpreted according to each country's domestic law and not according to international law. In contrast, Article 1(a) of the Charter gives a very precise definition of the regional or minority languages enjoying protection.

5.   The Charter thus covers a series of different situations, it being possible that States which do not recognise the existence of "national minorities" on their territory may accept the existence of one or more "regional languages".

b)   Differences *ratione materiae*

6.   The scope of the Framework Convention is broader, as it also takes account of religious and political factors. For instance:

    a)   Article 7 covers freedom of peaceful assembly, freedom of association, freedom of expression, and freedom of thought, conscience and religion;

    b)   Article 8 covers the right of persons belonging to national minorities to manifest their religion or beliefs and to establish religious institutions, organisations and associations;

    c)   Article 9 covers freedom of expression, including the freedom to hold opinions and to receive and impart information and ideas in a minority language;

    d)   Article 15 refers, *inter alia*, to effective participation in political affairs, in particular those affecting persons belonging to national minorities;

e) Article 17 deals with the participation by persons belonging to national minorities in non-governmental organisations at both national and international level.

These subjects are not covered by the Charter.

7. In other cases, the Framework Convention goes beyond the provisions of the Charter, for instance:

a) Article 5 (2) requires States to refrain from taking measures aimed at the assimilation of persons belonging to national minorities against their will (a provision of this kind is implied in the Charter);

b) Article 16 requires States to refrain from altering the proportions of the population in areas inhabited by persons belonging to national minorities, whereas Article 7(1) of the Charter confines itself to a more general reference to respect for such areas.

c) <u>Differences with regard to the types of protection</u>

8. In most cases, the individual articles of the Framework Convention do not lay down specific positive measures. As stated in the explanatory report (para 11), the Convention only sets out "programme-type provisions". It therefore falls to national legislation to translate the relevant principles into concrete provisions governing what should be done (introduction of protection or promotion measures, granting of facilities or rights to persons belonging to national minorities, etc) and what should be prevented (any interference with the exercise of particular activities by persons belonging to national minorities).

9. In contrast, the Charter provides for a more sophisticated system of protection:

a) Part II lays downs objectives and principles on which each Contracting Party must base its legislation and policies in respect of all the regional or minority languages used within its territory;

b) In respect of the languages specified at the time of ratification, each Contracting Party undertakes to apply a minimum of thirty-five paragraphs or sub-paragraphs chosen from among the provisions of Part III of the Charter, including at least three chosen from each of Articles 8 (education) and 12 (cultural activities and facilities) and one from each of Articles 9 (judicial authorities), 10 (administrative authorities and public services), 11 (media) and 13 (economic and social life). All the paragraphs and sub-paragraphs concerned set out positive measures for the protection and promotion of regional or minority languages which take the form of specific legal undertakings.

10. Despite their differences, the two instruments should be regarded as being complementary in the areas which they cover jointly:

- the Framework Convention lays down the general principles (in particular, that the protection of national minorities is a question of human rights) and indicates the areas in which protection measures are required, as well as the general outlines for such protection;

- the Charter proposes concrete measures which could give substance to the programme-type provisions set out in the Framework Convention and provide the "minimum threshold" of protection.

II. **COUNCIL OF EUROPE CONVENTIONS AND THE PROTECTION OF LOCAL AND REGIONAL AUTONOMY ("TERRITORIAL AUTONOMY")**

11. In the context of this conference, the central question is whether the two Council of Europe legal instruments described above or any other international texts drawn up within the Council actually provide a guarantee of "territorial autonomy".

12. For the purposes of this report, the latter term encompasses the two more specific concepts of "local self-government" and "regional self-government". To paraphrase the European Charter of Local Self-Government, it is taken here to mean the right and ability of local, county and regional authorities, within the limits of the law, to regulate and manage a substantial share of public affairs under their own responsibility and in the interests of the local population.

13. As such, it involves application of the principle of subsidiarity, which the European Charter of Local Self-Government defines as meaning that "public responsibilities shall generally be exercised, in preference, by those authorities which are closest to the citizen. Allocation of responsibility to another authority should weigh up the extent and nature of the task and requirements of efficiency and economy".

14. In domestic terms and in keeping with the views of Denis de Rougement, the concept of subsidiarity defined in this way encompasses the legal forms of federalism, regionalism and local self-government.

15. The Council of Europe instrument which guarantees local self-government is the European Charter of Local Self-Government, which has so far been ratified by twenty-one member States and signed by four. The Congress of Local and Regional Authorities of Europe (CLRAE) is currently drawing up a similar instrument concerning regional self-government.

a) Council of Europe Conventions

16. In fact, however, neither the European Charter of Local Self-Government nor the draft European Charter of Regional Self-Government specifically mentions minorities, so one must conclude that the two instruments protect local or regional self-government only insofar as it is already enjoyed by minorities. They cannot be interpreted as inviting States to grant minorities some degree of local or regional self-government.

17. We must therefore turn to the two legal instruments which the Council of Europe has produced on minorities, namely the Framework Convention for the Protection of National Minorities and the European Charter for Regional or Minority Languages, to see whether and to what extent they provide for the possibility of autonomous local or regional structures for minorities.

18. None of the articles of the Framework Convention deals with this issue. For its part, however, the European Charter for Regional or Minority Languages does include two references of a direct and indirect nature to the matter, namely in Article 7.1(b) and Article 10.

19.   Article 7.1(b), which is in Part II of the Charter and therefore applies to all the regional or minority languages spoken within the territory of individual States, concerns the well-known tendency on the part of certain States to change the boundaries of administrative areas or regions inhabited by large numbers of speakers of regional or minority languages in order to alter the population balance in favour of speakers of the national language.

20.   In particular, Article 7.1(b) requires the Contracting Parties to respect the geographical area of each regional or minority language in order to ensure that existing or new administrative divisions do not constitute an obstacle to the promotion of that language.   Although it does not refer to administrative divisions, the Framework Convention does, in Article 16, reinforce this principle by requiring the Contracting Parties to refrain from taking measures which alter the proportions of the population in areas inhabited by persons belonging to national minorities and are aimed at restricting the rights and freedoms flowing from the principles enshrined in the Convention.   Given that Article 5 of the European Charter of Local Self-Government also provides that changes in local authority boundaries shall not be made without prior consultation of the communities concerned, one may conclude that the existing instruments do indeed protect the territorial boundaries of local authorities with large minority populations.

21.   Article 10 of the European Charter for Regional or Minority Languages deals with the use of such languages in government, the public services and local and regional authorities. Paragraph 2 of the article regulates the use of such languages in local or regional authorities on whose territory the number of residents who speak regional or minority languages is such as to justify the measures proposed, in particular:

    a)   the use of regional or minority languages within the framework of the regional or local authority;

    b)   the possibility for users of regional or minority languages to submit oral or written applications in these languages;

    c)   the publication by regional authorities of their official documents also in the relevant regional or minority languages;

    d)   the publication by local authorities of their official documents also in the relevant regional or minority languages;

    e)   the use by regional authorities of regional or minority languages in debates in their assemblies, without excluding, however, the use of the official language(s) of the State;

    f)   the use by local authorities of regional or minority languages in debates in their assemblies, without excluding, however, the use of the official language(s) of the State;

    g)   the use or adoption, if necessary in conjunction with the name in the official language(s), of traditional and correct forms of place-names in regional or minority languages.

22.   Although Article 10 is therefore very specific, neither it nor the Charter as a whole covers the question of the right of speakers of regional or minority languages to have at their disposal local or regional authorities corresponding to the geographical areas in which they live.

b)   Parliamentary Assembly and Venice Commission texts

23.   In fact, only Parliamentary Assembly Recommendation 1201 (1993) on an additional protocol on the rights of national minorities to the European Convention on Human Rights and the proposal by the Venice Commission for a European Convention for the Protection of Minorities actually deal with this question.

24.   Article 14 (1) of the Venice Commission's proposal attempts to reach a compromise between the demands of minorities and the requirement for the territorial integrity of States. Without referring to the actual structure of States, which may therefore be unitary, decentralised or federal, it provides that "States shall favour the effective participation of minorities in public affairs, in particular in decisions affecting the regions where they live or in the matters affecting them". In addition, although making no reference to the powers of the various authorities within individual States, Article 14(2) provides that, "as far as possible, States shall take minorities into account when dividing the national territory into political and administrative sub-divisions, as well as into constituencies".

25.   As is made clear in the explanatory report on the Venice Commission's proposal, Article 14 does not only concern minorities present in high concentrations in particular areas, but may also apply to those whose distribution is more scattered. The term "region" is also to be understood in its geographical sense and not in a political, legal or administrative one. In other words, local or regional self-government for areas where a minority is in the majority is only one solution among others for ensuring the involvement of minorities in public life.

26.   In contrast, Article 11 of the additional protocol proposed by the Parliamentary Assembly in Recommendation 1201 (1993) is very specific and provides that, "in the regions where they are in a majority, the persons belonging to a national minority shall have the right to have at their disposal appropriate local or autonomous authorities or to have a special status, matching the specific historical and territorial situation and in accordance with the domestic legislation of the State". The principle is clear, but no practical action has been taken on the Assembly's recommendation.

27.   However, the question of the legal scope and implications of Article 11 of the proposed protocol has recently resurfaced in two ways:

   a)   the Parliamentary Assembly has asked the Venice Commission for Democracy through Law for an opinion on Article 11, and;

   b)   the treaties Hungary has signed with Slovakia and Romania both mention Assembly Recommendation 1201 among the international texts to be used in defining the rights of their respective minorities, and the treaty of 5 April 1995 between Hungary and Croatia also mentions the recommendation.

28.   With regard to Recommendation 1201 (1993), the Venice Commission has concluded that:

-       any attempt to interpret Article 11 should be particularly cautious, and;

-       as international law now stands, an extensive approach to the right of minorities to have at their disposal local or autonomous authorities is possible only if this is provided for in a binding international legal instrument, which is not the case here.

29.   With regard to the references in the above-mentioned treaties to Assembly Recommendation 1201, it should be noted that:

a)   upon ratifying the treaty of 28 March 1995, Slovakia declared that it had neither accepted nor included in the treaty any wording that recognised the establishment of autonomous structures on an ethnic basis;

b)   the appendix to the treaty between Hungary and Romania states that the Parties agree that Recommendation 1201 does not oblige them to grant a right to local self-government based on ethnic criteria;

c)   the treaty between Hungary and Croatia mentions Recommendation 1201 as a basis for assessing the principles enshrined in international instruments, but contains no specific provision allowing for autonomous local or regional structures. It does, however, include provisions aimed at fostering transfrontier co-operation and preventing local, regional and national electoral constituencies being changed in a manner that would place minorities at a disadvantage.

e)   Transfrontier co-operation

30.   A further aspect of local and regional self-government which is being used increasingly at the Council of Europe to help protect minorities is transfrontier co-operation.

31.   The Declaration adopted by the Heads of State and Government in Vienna on 18 October 1993 sets out three principles concerning transfrontier co-operation:

a)   the Heads of State and Government recognised the importance of transfrontier co-operation for the construction of a united Europe by declaring that "the creation of a tolerant and prosperous Europe does not depend only on co-operation between States. It also requires transfrontier co-operation between local and regional authorities, without prejudice to the constitution and the territorial integrity of each State. We urge the Organisation to pursue its work in this field and to extend it to co-operation between non-adjacent regions";

b)   the Heads of State and Government drew attention to the part transfrontier co-operation could play in bringing about peaceful settlements to problems concerning national minorities, which do tend to live in frontier regions;

c)   the Heads of State and Government stated that transfrontier co-operation can help to combat racism and intolerance by boosting confidence between peoples.

32.   In keeping with the above, Article 18(2) of the Framework Convention provides that, "where relevant, the Parties shall take measures to encourage transfrontier co-operation". The European Charter for Regional or Minority Languages is more specific here: Article 7.1(i) states that the Contracting Parties should promote "appropriate types of transnational exchanges" and Article 14(b) then provides that, for the benefit or regional or minority languages, the Parties should "facilitate and/or promote co-operation across borders, in particular between regional or local authorities in whose territory the same language is used in identical or similar form".

III.   CONCLUSIONS

33.   The conclusion that must be drawn from this review of Council of Europe texts is that no legally binding instrument currently deals directly with the question of granting linguistic or other minorities local or regional self-government ("territorial autonomy").

34.   Nevertheless, closer examination of the European Charter for Regional or Minority Languages in its entirety and of certain individual provisions (Articles 10(2), 11(3) and 14(2)) of the Framework Convention indicates that the idea does underlie the protection measures proposed.

35.   The Charter as a whole and the above-mentioned articles of the Framework Convention base the protection provided on a territorial principle: the protection and promotion measures are to be implemented in the areas where the regional or minority languages are spoken.

36.   Although this consistent reference to the areas in which regional or minority languages are spoken does place a geographical limit on the application of the Charter, it also confirms that the area or territory in question is the geographical, legal and administrative framework in which the protection measures must be implemented. This interpretation is reinforced by the importance attached in the Charter to transfrontier co-operation.

37.   Similarly, the Venice Commission's opinion and the reference to Assembly Recommendation 1201 in the treaties Hungary has signed with Croatia, Slovakia and Romania can be interpreted as meaning that the Commission and the individual States, while stating that minorities have no right under international law to local or regional self-government ("territorial autonomy"), do recognise that the latter is indeed a possible means for ensuring the effective protection of minorities.

38.   These factors lay behind the CLRAE's decision to hold this conference with a view to determining the potential which such self-government offers here in the light of examples of autonomous structures enjoyed by minorities at regional, county and local level.

39.   Before this potential can be realised, however, it will be necessary to clear up the misunderstandings that persist not only in central and eastern Europe, but also in certain western countries regarding the concept itself. The type of self-government or autonomy involved here does not mean independence, but the exercise at local level, within the limits of the law and without prejudice to the territorial integrity of the State, of certain exclusive, shared or devolved powers.

40.   It should also be noted that it is not essential for all local or regional authorities within a given State to enjoy the same degree or form of self-government. Indeed, experience in Europe shows that, depending on particular circumstances of varying kinds (historical or cultural traditions, geographical or economic situations, high concentrations of minorities), some local and regional authorities may have more powers and responsibilities than others. The presence of linguistic or other minorities may be

regarded as such a circumstance, but it is not the only ground on which special powers or responsibilities may be granted.

41.   In conclusion, it seems to me that local or regional autonomy, involving either the establishment of local or regional authorities with appropriate powers or the development of transfrontier co-operation, now has a key role to play not only in promoting local democracy within the Council of Europe, but also in contributing to the effective protection of minorities in Europe.

42.   If this conference were to confirm the possibilities offered by local and regional self-government in terms of helping to solve the problem of minorities, the idea of drafting a recommendation on the matter, mentioned in Section III, para 7, of CLRAE Resolution 232 (1992), would indeed be an initiative worthy of the attention of the Congress.

Ms Kristina WIKBERG,
Head of the Swedish-speaking Secretariat of the Association of Finnish Local Authorities and Vice-Chairman of the City Board of Espoo (Finland)

Minorities and local authorities.
Local autonomy of the Finnish municipalities of Swedish language

I am grateful and honoured for the opportunity given to me to present the background, the everyday life and the reality of the Swedish-speaking municipalities in Finland. It also pleases me that a conference with this very important topic is organised. To present a series of experiences of local and regional government institutions, which have been successfully used to solve the problems of minorities, will most certainly be useful and give good advice for the ongoing European integration. On the basis of these experiences we can perhaps find ways to solve the problems faced by minorities in Eastern and Central Europe.

As an introduction I want to state that the Finnish way of defining to which language group one belongs, in many ways differs from that of several other countries. The Finnish way of defining language groups is strongly referring to the individual. A Finnish citizen is registered as Finnish-speaking or Swedish-speaking in accordance with the information he or she gives about himself or herself. Thus, the Finnish system of linguistic rights has a firm basis in the rights of the individual. But at the same time it has elements of collective rights in the way the municipalities fulfil their responsibility for bilingualism. Finland also has experience of minority rights on a purely territorial basis, in the case of the autonomous region of the Åland islands.

Finland today is a country with two language groups living side by side in peace and harmony. Finnish as well as Swedish are recognized as national languages. The legal basis for our country's bilingualism is in the Constitutional law. I will come back to this topic later on.

I believe that the Finnish experiences can be of great interest in every discussion about minority languages and individual rights, collective rights of groups or practical ways of finding working solutions or compromises between these.

Historical background

To understand the language situation and the status of the Swedish-speaking municipalities one needs to know the general historical background of Finland and the Swedish-speaking part of the population.

Finland has throughout its recorded history been a bilingual country. From ancient times Swedish-speaking people have lived along the coastline of the country. From the time of the crusades in the 12th century until 1809 when Russia conquered the country, Finland was an integral part of Sweden. During this time, Swedish culture made a lasting imprint on every branch of the country's life. Culturally and politically, if not geographically, Finland belongs to Scandinavia.

Swedish became the predominant language of the educated classes, the administration and the courts. The situation was not altered by the Russian conquest. Finland was given an autonomous status within the Russian Empire, and internal affairs were not radically changed. In the middle of the 19th century, Finland was also influenced by nationalist movements, and the struggle for the Finnish language began. Between 1863 and 1902 the privileged position of the Swedish language was gradually abolished in favour of equality between the two languages.

The period of linguistic strife continued from about 1880 to the Second World War. The crucial moment came when Finland became independent in 1917. In Finland's Constitution Act of 1919 the country was defined as a republic with two languages. The Second World War finally strongly united the people of Finland, regardless of language.

It is important to recognize that the national identity of the Swedish-speaking Finns is linked to Finland and not to Sweden. We recognize Swedish as our mother tongue, but Finland as our country. The historical ties between Finland and Sweden can though still be seen as we have similar administrative structures and similar values.

Some facts about Finland and the municipalities

Finland is a bilingual republic with about 5 million inhabitants. The Finnish-speaking part of the population has always been the majority. Today we have about 300 000 persons, or 6 per cent who speak Swedish as their mother tongue. The social structure of the Swedish-speaking population is generally very similar to that of the entire population.

Almost all the Swedish-speaking population is today, as earlier, concentrated along the southern and western coasts of Finland. A great part of the rural areas and some of the costal towns in these regions are strongly Swedish-dominated. In some of the bigger cities, e.g. Esbo, where I come from, the Swedish-speaking people live in Finnish-speaking or bilingual surroundings.

In Finland the number of municipalities totals to 452. The population of the municipalities vary from the half a million of the capital Helsinki to municipalities with a population of a few hundred. If the unilingual Finnish-speaking municipalities are left out when dividing the municipalities according to their language status, there are today:

- 21 unilingual Swedish-speaking municipalities
- 22 bilingual municipalities with Swedish as the majority language
- 21 bilingual municipalities with Finnish as the majority language

In Finland the municipalities have the main responsibility for the social welfare and the provision of basic services to their residents. Finland has no elected regional administration. Instead municipalities cooperate in the provision of many vital services. Hospitals, for instance, are often run by establishing joint municipal authorities.

The municipalities in Finland run comprehensive schools, upper secondary schools and vocational institutes. They provide adult education, library services, cultural and leisure services. They are also responsible for providing child daycare, care for the elderly and the disabled, socially targeted housing and income support for those in need. They run health centres that provide primary and secondary health care and dental services. They supervise land use and building activities within their areas. To finance all this, the municipalities have the right to tax their residents.

Constitutional provisions and legal framework of linguistic rights

The fundamental provisions concerning the status of the Swedish and Finnish languages are found in Section 14 of the Constitution Act. Section 14 of the fundamental rights was revised one year ago, in the summer of 1995, and it reads:

"The national languages of Finland shall be Finnish and Swedish.

The right of everyone to use his own language, whether Finnish or Swedish, as a party in proceedings before a court of law or other authority, and to obtain document from them in that language, shall be guaranteed by Act of Parliament. Public authorities shall take care to provide for the educational, cultural and social needs of the Finnish-speaking and the Swedish-speaking populations of the country according to similar principles."

The Sami as an indigenous people as well as the Romanies and other groups shall have the right to maintain and develop their own languages and cultures. Provisions governing the right of the Sami to use the Sami language before the public authorities shall be prescribed by Act of the Parliament. The rights of those who use sign language and those who require interpretation or translation because of a disability shall be guaranteed by Act of Parliament.

The first paragraph, declaring Finnish and Swedish to be the national languages, clearly treats them as languages on an equal basis. Although the paragraph may be considered rather a moral and political principle than a law for immediate application, all Finnish language legislation, including the legislation relating to municipalities, rests on it.

The second paragraph, which states that the right of everyone to use his own language, whether Finnish or Swedish, as a party in proceedings before a court of law or other authority, and to obtain document from them in that language, shall be guaranteed by Act of Parliament must be carried into effect in accordance with principles of equality. Laws and decrees, Government proposals to Parliament and Parliament⌐s replies, petitions, recommendations, as well as other official communications to and from the Government, shall be drawn up in Finnish and Swedish.

The second paragraph also states that public authorities shall take care to provide for the educational, cultural and social needs of the Finnish-speaking and the Swedish-speaking populations of the country according to similar principles. This may be considered the basis for providing the citizens similar public services, regardless of their mother tongue. This has e.g. implication and great significance when building up networks and services in education, media and health care.

As to the Constitution Act I also wish to refer to its Section 50, which in regard to the division of the general administration prescribes as follows:

In any rearrangement of the boundaries of administrative districts, care shall be taken that, where circumstances permit, the districts are monolingual, either Finnish-speaking or Swedish-speaking, or that their linguistic minorities are as small as possible.

Over the years this rule has become more difficult to follow as the lingually mixed areas have increased, but it has been of great importance as the moral basis for trying to draw boundaries so that the minorities are concentrated and provide for the practical arrangements of services. The right for the conscripts to perform their military service in their own language is also found here, which has provided the grounds for establishing a special brigade for Swedish-speaking conscripts. The Church is also lingually divided.

The principles laid down in the Constitution have been developed in other Acts, in particular in the Language Act, which is of vital importance in regard to how the linguistic division is carried into effect in the municipalities and consequently also on the obligations of the municipalities to provide services in the minority language.

The municipalities and their duty to provide services in the minority language

The basic unit for providing services to the citizens in Finland is the municipality. The language status of the municipality determines its obligations towards its residents. In a unilingual municipality the authorities only have to use the municipality⌐s language, Finnish or Swedish. In bilingual cases needs have to be met according to the principles of equality. This does not, however, affect the fact that all citizens have the right to use their own language as a party before the courts or in their dealing with other state authorities,
irrespective of the linguistic character of the district.

According to law municipalities can be either unilingual or bilingual. The municipality is unilingual when the minority, either Swedish-speaking or Finnish-speaking, is less than 8 per cent or 3 000 persons. If the minority exceeds these figures, the municipality becomes bilingual. In order to avoid the influence of occasional shifts, a bilingual municipality does not become unilingual until the minority has decreased under 6 per cent. The linguistic status of the municipalities is corrected, if necessary, every ten years by the State Government. The linguistic status of larger administrative units, for instance hospital districts, is determined by the municipalities that form the joint municipal authority. If there is even one bilingual municipality, the larger unit is also regarded as bilingual.

Before I enter into describing the main ways of safeguarding the continued existence of the Swedish-speaking population in Finland for the years ahead, I will briefly tell you about the Åland islands.

The Åland islands - an example of a purely territorial way to define linguistic rights

The province of Åland, is declared to be a unilingual region in Finland, where the predominance of the Swedish language and culture are guaranteed by law. The Åland islands and the municipalities there are a remarkable exception to the principle of equality of both the national languages. This special status has its own historical background. At the beginning of the 20th century the people of Åland wanted their islands to be a part of Sweden which resulted in an international conflict. The conflict was solved by the League of Nations in 1921 giving Finland the sovereignty of the islands, but requesting Finland to give Åland an autonomous status with guarantees for the Swedish language.

Today Åland manages a great deal of its own internal affairs, and very few people living in the area show interest in turning to Sweden any more.

Åland is an example of a purely territorial definition of the rights of a language group.

Education and other linguistic obligations

The language question has been extremely important in the field of education. As in the other Nordic countries education is one of the most important tasks of the municipalities.   The Finnish education system is made up of comprehensive school, secondary post-comprehensive general education and vocational education, tertiary education and various forms of adult education. One of the main strengths of the Swedish-speaking people has always been their own educational school system and at the municipal level, a separate educational administration.

I want to point out and stress that our educational system, which is autonomous and covering almost all levels and disciplines, with its instruction and teaching in Swedish, is the cornerstone of our culture.

In particular in the regions with a predominance of Finnish, the Swedish schools safeguard the continuance of the Swedish-speaking population. Many young bilingual families, in which the mother and the father speak different languages, have also understood this and chosen a Swedish school for their children. This is a trend that gives hope for the future.

Besides education there are several provisions in our legislation that give citizens the right to services in their mother tongue, Finnish or Swedish. One example worth mentioning is that patients are entitled to health care in their mother tongue. This has proved to be of particular interest to three categories of patients: children, elderly and psychiatric patients.

The future of the Swedish-speaking Finns

In comparison with most other multilingual and multicultural countries the language climate is very good in today's Finland. After the Second World War the language strife can be mentioned only as something that has appeared on newspaper pages or in political contexts.

Also in everyday life there is a lot of contacts over the language boundaries, the Swedish-speaking Finns command and use their mother tongue. In spite of an increasing bilingualism, the knowledge of the minority language has not as yet been lost. About one third of all Swedish-speaking Finns can be said to be unilingual, the rest knows the Finnish language and also uses it in various degrees in their everyday life and at work.

The maintenance of the minority language calls for active measures on various levels of society. One prerequisite is the consciousness of the own culture and its fragility. The good will of the legislator is another. Still, the most important precondition is a good language climate in which the majority comprehends that different languages and cultures are a richness to the country.

Ladies and Gentlemen,

I have tried to convey my views on minority languages and local autonomy based on my own experiences and views as head of the Swedish-speaking Secretariat of the Association of Finnish Local Authorities and as elected municipal official and Vice-Chairman of the City Board of Esbo, the second biggest, bilingual municipality in Finland.

In Finland we have the individual right of recording and determining one's own language combined with the obligation of the collective and the municipality to safeguard the interests of the minority. I hope that our positive experience can be of use in other parts of Europe as well.

I thank you for your attention.

Mr Jean-Marie WOEHRLING,
President of the Administrative Tribunal, Strasbourg (France)

The legal status of Alsace-Moselle

CONTENTS

A comparative study of the different types of local regulations which exist to protect regional cultures reveals the case of Alsace to be something of a paradox: in accordance with the unitary principles which dominate the organisation of French public institutions, there are no specific regulations for Alsace; however, specific legal arrangements do exist for Alsace-Lorraine. Consequently, although Alsace has no special set of regulations, it is at the same time an example of a very specific legal situation in the context of France as a whole. We could say that, like the doctor in Molière's play, this state of affairs has come about by accident rather than design.

In order to understand the legal situation of Alsace, we must begin with the French institutional framework, go on to recall the historical context in which Alsace's specific regime took shape, then study the present-day legal situation of this region and, finally, speculate on the prospects for development of the local laws of Alsace-Moselle.

I.   The French institutional framework

It is widely known that France is a unitary state. This principle of unity has its basis in the Constitution, but on a more fundamental level, it corresponds to an ideological view. It is in sharp contrast with the existence of local law, specific to a very small part of the national territory.

A.   The ideological basis for the French principle of institutional unity

The philosophical position which still prevails in France today tends towards a standardising and individualistic interpretation of the principles of liberty and equality. This is consistent with a coherent and all-embracing philosophy which has been developing since the demise of the *Ancien Régime.*

In the context of this philosophy the two poles of political life are the State, on the one hand, and the citizen, on the other. Any intermediary institution, group or community can represent a threat to the coherence of the State and to individual freedoms. Indeed, the recognition of a law as being specific to one group constitutes an element of discrimination against individuals who are not members of that group and challenges the unity of the State. Consequently, any affirmation of an identity can only result from individual and voluntary action, not from membership of a group. While the individual is protected from the State by the principles of freedom and equality, the State is also a guarantor for the individual: compared with the feudal, provincial or corporatist structures of the *Ancien Régime,* the State represents progress and freedom; it is the framework within which the individual can freely determine himself in relation to ideological, economic, territorial, religious or other structures. Conversely, groups of a professional, ethnic, religious or other nature constitute a potential threat to individual freedom because they are a differentiating factor likely to strike a blow at equality and because, by their very nature, they take a particularist view which is more philosophically, intellectually and socially limited. In other words, the highest form of collectivity - the State - is best able to guarantee freedom, intellectual openness and social progress. Structures which are narrower, whether on a territorial or other scale, cannot fail to be more restrictive of individual potential, be it political, philosophical, economic or social.

Based on such an analysis, there is a long tradition of confidence in the general institutions of the State, its administration, its training and its intellectual leaders with a corresponding mistrust of local structures and all types of particularism whether religious, linguistic, cultural or otherwise. These are suspected, with varying degrees of openness, of obscurantism, insularity, political or social regression, irrationality, a desire to discriminate and even various forms of corruption.

The constitutional and administrative principles of French institutions are based on this ideological view, which clearly does not favour certain parts of national territory being granted regional autonomy.

B. The Constitutional framework for French institutions

Article 2 of the Constitution of 4 October 1958 states: "France is an indivisible, secular, democratic and social Republic. It ensures the equality before the law of all citizens, without distinction of origin, race or religion. It respects all beliefs". It is on the basis of this provision which is, in itself, quite general and open to a wide variety of interpretations, that centralist philosophical views find their legal expression. Traditionally, the principles of equality and secularity are interpreted by the uniformisation of public institutions and individual rights. It was not until recently that attempts were made to impose different interpretations.

The desire to ensure the equality of all French citizens in an indivisible Republic makes any reference to a right to be different pointless, or even impossible. Since France ensures the equality of all before the law, without distinction, it cannot acknowledge the existence of minorities on its territory. The exercise of universally-acknowledged freedoms and the normal democratic process form an exclusive framework for the expression of specificities, be they cultural, religious or regional.

In line with this particular interpretation of its constitutional order, whenever the occasion has arisen France has been obliged to state that there are no minorities on its territory. For instance it has entered a reservation with regard to article 27 of the International Covenant on Civil and Political Rights. Under the terms of this article, in states where minorities exist, members of such minorities cannot be deprived of the right, in common with other members of their group, to their own cultural life, to profess and practise their own religion and to use their own language. France has stated that, in view of article 2 of its Constitution, the aforementioned article 27 would not be applicable on its territory. According to such an analysis, ethnic, linguistic, cultural and religious minorities cannot exist in France because all citizens are equal; consequently there is no call for any provision relating to the protection of minorities. An identical reservation accompanied France's accession to the Convention on the Rights of the Child signed in New York on 26 January 1990 with regard to article 30 of the Convention, according to which in States where minorities or persons of indigenous origin exist, a child belonging to such a minority may not be deprived of the right to his own cultural life and to use his own language in common with the other members of his group. France considered that this provision was not applicable in France since it did not recognise minorities.

In its interventions in international debates, France has always defended the position that the protection of minorities is assured in the first place by the effective development of democracy and by the application of rules relating to the protection of human rights. It has constantly refused to be bound by documents or international declarations which would enable territorial, ethnic or religious minorities to exercise any rights peculiar to them. This is strongly criticised by the regional and linguistic minorities which do, in fact, exist in France and which, as a result of this reasoning, are unable to benefit from the protective principles enshrined in such international documents.

The same rules of interpretation in favour of uniform organisation apply to the administrative organisation of the country. France is divided into regions, *départements* and communes; the institutional organisation within each of these categories of local authority is the same, regardless of the local situation: basically, a commune with ten inhabitants will have the same institutional framework as a city with one million. According to a decision of the Constitutional Council of 2 December 1982, the same constitutional rules must apply to all local collectivities belonging to the same category. The territorial and administrative organisation of France is therefore conceived according to a principle of uniformity which has the same legal framework throughout the country, regardless of ethnic, demographic, economic and geographical or spatial considerations. The map of the different *départements*, drawn at the time of the Revolution, aimed to divide the country into a hundred districts of similar dimensions, delineated according to general and abstract criteria. The principle of equality applies within each category of local authority just as it applies among citizens. It is therefore hardly consistent with this line of thinking to grant a particular local authority a status of its own which differs from the status of other local authorities of the same category.

The exercise of civil rights cannot vary from one part of the territory to another, so the fundamental guarantees in respect of such civil rights must be given by the state authorities: local authorities cannot have any significant influence on the implementation of civil rights because this could result in differences in the implementation of civil rights depending on the priorities of such authorities. For example, the organisation of the civil right of education does not allow local authorities any discretion in the financing of private schools because if they did this right would no longer be uniformly assured throughout the country (Constitutional Council, ruling No 93-329 DC of 13 January 1994).

In a similar vein, the French principle of secularity goes beyond the concept of the neutrality of the State in terms of religion. It is understood as an indifference on the part of the State with regard to religious activities. The respect of religious beliefs is passive, rather than by providing a status or institutional framework for each individual belief, since such action is seen as going beyond the principle of equality and neutrality. The concept of the neutrality of public institutions results in a clear distinction being made between the public and private spheres. Religious, linguistic, ethnic or cultural considerations come exclusively within the private domain and cannot, therefore, be the subject of any form of recognition or be afforded any organisational framework in the public domain. Neutrality and equality with regard to all these considerations results in an indifference to every one of them. They cannot claim any privileges other than those which belong to each individual in his private sphere. It is only when individual rights are in danger of being compromised that such considerations are taken into account in the organisation of the administration and in the workings of public services.

The recent insertion in article 2 of the Constitution of the fact that French is the language of the Republic also implies a refusal to take account of specific regional linguistic considerations. In a recent ruling (No 96-373 DC of 9 April 1996) the Constitutional Council considered that, in view of this constitutional provision, no law could provide for the Polynesian language to be used concurrently with French in the public services in Polynesia nor could that language be made a compulsory subject in state schools.

Where political institutions are concerned, it is the normal working of democratic institutions which must constitute the framework for the expression of particularisms. At the level of central institutions there is no specific representation of local or regional structures. Members of parliament are the elected representatives of all citizens and not the representatives of specific regional or cultural bodies. Although Parliament's second chamber, the Senate, is deemed specifically to represent local authorities, this is more as a result of custom than a specific status for these structures within this chamber.

However, contemporary legal scholars point out that the principle of the unity of the Republic is not, as such, sanctioned by the Constitution; as for indivisibility, what this actually signifies is the indivisibility of sovereignty, that is to say the unconstitutionality of the implementation of a federal order, but not indivisibility as far as organisation of the legal system is concerned. For instance, some elements of territorial diversification have been sanctioned. These benefit, in particular, the Overseas *départements* and territories which, under the terms of the Constitution itself, may be granted specific status. More recently, constitutional case-law had permitted geographical, economic or cultural differences to be taken into account to justify the creation of specific categories of local authority. For instance, the granting of a status specific to Corsica was deemed to be constitutional, the only exception being a provision referring to the existence of a Corsican people, a concept which was deemed to be incompatible with the existence of the French people. In the context of practical arrangements, specific regimes have been developed for some local authorities (the status of the city of Paris, particular electoral regimes for the cities of Paris, Lyons and Marseilles, planning legislation specifically applicable to coastal or mountain areas, etc.). There are, therefore, the beginnings of a pluralist interpretation of article 2 of the Constitution and of a wider applicability of article 72, which refers to the free administration of local authorities. However, this is a recent and relatively tentative trend. Some commentators speak of progression from a denial of the existence of any difference to the management of such differences.

The discussion of local Alsace-Moselle law is one facet of this progressive acceptance in French law of geographical or cultural differences. The issue of the constitutionality of a law applicable only to a fraction of French territory has been raised. It no longer appears to be rejected out of hand, but certain local laws are still quite frequently deemed to be unconstitutional. This is particularly true of regulations under local law which interfere with individual freedoms since, according to some interpreters of the Constitution, these ought to be uniformly regulated throughout the national territory. Such views have not, however, been followed by the courts, in spite of the fact that they have the power to give the later (constitutional) law precedence over the earlier (local) law.

II.   The historical origin of a law specifically applicable to Alsace-Moselle

The existence of a legal framework specific to Alsace-Moselle is not the result of a desire to confer a particular status on that region; it is merely the result of the failure to reintegrate this territory fully into the French legal system after it was returned to France in 1918. At that time, it was the aim of the French authorities to eradicate any trace of German annexation as quickly as possible and to reintegrate Alsace-Lorraine into French institutions as completely as possible. This desire was particularly keen because the legal and administrative institutions of the territory at that time were not seen as a regional peculiarity, but as the result of German occupation and consequently as a mark of the occupier which had to be erased as quickly as possible. The existence of linguistic, cultural or religious differences, if anyone was aware of them, was systematically underestimated and such differences were themselves perceived to be a consequence of the German occupation rather than the manifestation of an individual identity. Even in this respect, it was not considered necessary to take particular account of this identity, which would have to be thrown into the French institutional melting pot along with every other regional identity throughout the country. As a result, Alsace-Lorraine was once more to be divided into three ordinary *départements* as soon as this could be achieved. This was the method which had been used to return other territories to France (Nice in 1864 and Savoie in 1862).

These aims were achieved fairly quickly on an institutional level. However another solution prevailed with regard to the question of applicable law, and this was the progressive and selective introduction of French legislation.

A. Institutional standardisation

In terms of institutional organisation, Alsace-Moselle rapidly became part of the French institutional framework and, in parallel with this, the majority of the region's local institutions which had existed prior to 1918 disappeared. As soon as the recovered territories were occupied by French troops, the fundamental rules of French administrative organisation were introduced. An Act of 17 October 1919 on transitional arrangements for Alsace-Lorraine conferred legality on such measures. Three *départements* were reconstituted in the former Reichsland, at the head of each of which was appointed a *Commissaire de la République* (Commissioner) carrying out the duties of the *Préfet* (Prefect). These three Commissioners were not, however, attached directly to the Ministry of the Interior, but placed under the authority of a Commissioner General, a "regional" authority with the rank of Minister, whose first incumbent was Alexandre Millerand, who saw this type of organisation as an experiment which could serve as a model for the future regionalisation of France. To some extent this post of Commissioner General of Alsace-Lorraine reflected the survival of the former pre-1919 Ministry of Alsace-Lorraine, with the Commissioner General acting, like the *Statthalter*, directly under the authority of the President of the *Conseil des Ministres* (Cabinet), with all departments associated with the administrations of Alsace and Lorraine coming under his authority. The Commissioner General was assisted by a consultative organ, whose original title of *Conseil supérieur d'Alsace et de Lorraine* was later changed to *Conseil consultatif d'Alsace et de Lorraine*. By virtue of an Act of 17 October 1919, this had all but legislative powers, since it had the responsibility of deciding by Order either to introduce French legislation, or to revoke local laws.

It had, however, always been intended that the arrangements with regard to the office of Commissioner General would be transitional. The arrangements were destined to come to an end, either when the organisational arrangements applicable to the rest of France were extended to Alsace-Lorraine, or when regionalisation made it possible to generalise the experiment. As it did not prove possible to implement such a reform, the office of Commissioner General became an institution whose aim was to do away with itself by working towards assimilation, which would render it unnecessary. This assimilation work progressed rapidly and took the form of successive transfers of departments answerable to the Commissioner to corresponding ministries in Paris. This gradually reduced the size of the office of the Commissioner General, which was finally abolished by an Act of 24 July 1925. This Act reintegrated Alsace-Moselle almost completely into the administrative framework of ordinary law. Prefects were re-established with their usual title and powers; administrative departments functioned as elsewhere in France, except that a *Direction générale d'Alsace-Lorraine* was created in Paris under the authority of the President of the *conseil des ministres*, to which were attached a number of services of the three *départements* which had not been attached to a particular ministry; this *direction générale* itself disappeared immediately after the Second World War. Consequently, from 1925 onwards the only surviving elements of the administrative structure peculiar to the former Alsace-Lorraine were a department of ecclesiastical matters, a social security bureau and an administrative court for Alsace-Lorraine. Total unification was achieved for all public services: railways, postal services, state education, the courts, etc. In terms of organisation, these services were managed as in other *départements*, with none of the structures of the former Alsace-Lorraine surviving. In the political sphere, common electoral laws had been introduced from 1919 onwards and the inhabitants of the three *départements* were represented by the existing institutions (Parliament, *département* councils and district councils) with no specific structure for the recovered territories.

B.   Harmonisation of laws

Unification with regard to applicable substantive law was a more gradual process and is still not complete.   At the time of disannexation the French authorities decided that the recovered *départements* would continue to be governed temporarily by the legislation in force at the time until such time as the corresponding French legislation was introduced.   This decision to retain pre-1919 legislation was not the result of a desire to respect the peculiar nature of the disannexed provinces, but was rather made necessary by political and practical considerations and on the understanding that it would be no more than temporary.

There were a number of reasons for the temporary retention of German laws: in the first place, the legislation of Alsace-Moselle in some sectors (social security, company law, land registry, powers of the commune) was more modern and technically superior to French legislation, so that the application of the latter would have been a genuine step backwards for Alsace-Lorraine.   Moreover, French lawmakers at that time had plans to make speedy changes to a number of laws which were deemed to be unsatisfactory.   It would serve no purpose to introduce in the three *départements* legislation seen to be in need of modification.   In some areas, German law had, in addition, drawn up comprehensive legislation which had no equivalent in France (insurance law, professional codes, social security, etc).   Such provisions could not be revoked unless others existed to replace them.   In other sectors, the introduction of French law would have caused excessive harm to the interests of certain professions or branches of the economy (lawyers, notaries, etc.).   A number of transitional arrangements and adaptive measures were therefore necessary.

These "rational" considerations were not the only - or even the most important - reasons for the attachment of the population of the recovered provinces to "their" local law.   Above all, they were anxious to maintain certain fundamental principles which were prominent features of society in Alsace-Moselle and which would have been threatened by the total introduction of French law.   First and foremost among these principles was the religious status of the recovered *départements* and the place of religion in schools.   Alongside the issue of religion, there was also the organisation of certain professions, principally craft trades and the existence of communal powers.   It is issues such as this, often qualified as "local exemptions", which have caused a good deal of heated discussion about local law.

The French authorities therefore agreed to a progressive introduction of French law, using a variety of methods depending on the subject-matter.   As local laws were only intended to continue in force for a relatively short time, little thought was given to the theoretical and practical implications of the continuing existence of such laws.   The only practical step provided for by two Acts dated 1 June 1924 was the publication of an official translation of the legislation remaining in force.   However, this principle was only partially implemented.

During the early years after disannexation, there were many measures to introduce French legislation, covering a large number of administrative institutions, social law, criminal law and some elements of tax law.   The uncertain nature of the duration of their applicability was determined with the adoption of two important Acts of 1 June 1924 introducing civil and commercial legislation.   These two Acts reaffirmed the principle of the provisional nature of maintaining in force the legal regime of the three recovered *départements* by setting a time limit of ten years for the unification process.   This deadline was, however, renewed several times before it was finally decided to abandon any idea of a precise time limit.

After the introduction of the two above-mentioned Acts of 1924, the pace of legislative unification slowed down, only to gather speed slightly after the Second World War. A number of important unification measures have also be introduced recently. In all, a large proportion of French legislation has been introduced in this way in the *départements* of Alsace and Moselle. Nevertheless, in a number of important sectors local legislation remains in force and even though these exceptions may appear to be limited compared to French legislation as a whole, they do represent a notable exception to the principle of legislative unity throughout French territory and concern a number of not unimportant issues.

III. The content of local law in Alsace-Moselle in the present day

The legislation which remains in force in Alsace-Lorraine appears to be comprised of successive layers, the application of each of which is beset by particular problems:

- old, pre-1870 French law, maintained in force successively after 1870 and 1918;

- German federal law, applicable throughout Germany and maintained in force in Alsace-Moselle after 1918;

- legislation which is specifically applicable in Reichsland Elsass-Lothringen alone, drawn up during the period of annexation between 1870 and 1918 by local legislative and regulatory bodies;

- provisions specific to Alsace-Lorraine adopted after 1918 by the lawmaker or by French regulatory authority; in fact, the French public authorities were themselves obliged to develop a "new" local law, known as "third legislation", in areas where it did not seem appropriate either to preserve the old local law, or to introduce general French law.

Today this local law does not constitute a coherent whole, but a collection of ad hoc measures of varying importance. Furthermore, the rules governing its use in conjunction with general law are not always clear.

A. *The scope of local law*

The following are the principal areas where local laws survive:

-arrangements concerning religion: 19th century French legislation, as amended by the German authorities, remains in force. The principal features are that it distinguishes between, on the one hand, recognised religions, which have a particular status under public law and benefit from various advantages, such as the remuneration of ministers of religion, in exchange for specific guarantees to the authorities and, on the other hand, unrecognised religions which may be freely practised but which do not benefit from any particular advantage or specific assistance, although the possibility of subsidies does exist. Religious education is organised in primary and secondary schools;

- arrangements concerning craft trades: these are governed by the Professional Code, which is German in origin. It includes a definition of craft trades which differs from the definition under French law, and which, based on the means of production, permits the status of craft trade to be granted to relatively large undertakings. These provisions also include arrangements for the organisation of apprenticeships and provide for the existence of groups of specific crafts people: (voluntary or mandatory trade guilds);

- social legislation: this is characterised by the existence of a type of compulsory complementary social security scheme which offers insured persons in the three *départements* specific services financed by higher contributions. There are also specific rules which apply to agricultural accident insurance, pension schemes and social assistance;

- business and labour law: the three *départements* have specific rules concerning Sunday rest days and public holidays. The professional code referred to above also includes a variety of rules for the administrative control of some occupations. Some local regulations guarantee private sector employees full salary without either a period of grace or conditions of seniority in cases of absence for which they are not responsible. Other specific measures relate to commercial law, such as the agreement not to enter into competition;

- local hunting regulations: local hunting legislation, which is very similar to German law, continues in force: hunting rights have been withdrawn from landowners and are administered by the commune, which invites bids for them every nine years. The hunting rights are awarded to the highest bidder, who must pay a rent for them and, in addition, must comply with a hunting plan. A specific procedure and regulations govern the making good of damage caused by game;

- local arrangements governing associations: German law governing clubs and associations as provided for in articles 21 and 79 of the German Civil Code remains in force; it confers on associations registered with the district court a more comprehensive legal personality than associations formed under French law;

- notification of information relating to real estate: this is not organised by the Ministry of Finance, as it is in the rest of France, but by means of a land register kept by a specialist law officer who is responsible to the Ministry of Justice. Registration in the land register implies the existence of a property right. The land register may be consulted directly by the general public.

In addition to the abovementioned sectors, specific legislation still exists governing some aspects of the organisation of the courts and local communal law as well as in a number of areas of secondary importance.

It is clear, then, that local law is only of marginal relevance to issues of regional significance in cultural or linguistic matters. There is, in particular, hardly any local legislation relating to the use of languages or to bilingualism. When the three *départements* were returned to France, an Order of the President of the *Conseil des ministres* of 2 February 1919 determined that the language of the courts in Alsace and Lorraine would be French. Proceedings could be conducted in local dialect or in German if the president of the court so decided, but only if all persons involved declared that they could only speak the local dialect or German and that they had insufficient knowledge of French. The same Order of 2 February 1919 also imposed the use of French for notarial acts. However, case-law has deemed this obligation cannot validly be enforced.

Restrictive measures concerning the use of the German language in newspapers had been taken after the Second World War. Such provisions ought to have been considered no longer to apply after the suppression of wartime legislation, but the newspapers continued to apply them quite strictly. They were finally revoked formally by an Act of 1984. No specific local provisions exist with regard to radio and television. Only specifications applicable to the whole of France made a vague reference to regional languages. At the present time, regional television broadcasts programmes in Alsatian dialect for approximately two hours a week. In the field of education there is no more specific legislation in favour of the regional language or of bilingualism. The so-called Deixonne Act of 11 January 1951 on the teaching of local languages and dialect was not made applicable in Alsace-Moselle. In 1952 a decree was issued providing for the option to organise the teaching of German in primary schools, but it was hardly ever applied. Since 1975, a number of circulars issued by the chief education officer have been issued to organise basic German language classes in primary schools, but these circulars are merely internal administrative instructions and as such have no legal force. The result is that they cannot be regarded as creating rights for the benefit of users. Furthermore, their scope is limited because until quite recently they were restricted to providing for one to two hours' German teaching in the final years of primary school. It is only in the last two or three years that more intensive German teaching, in the form of bilingual classes where each language is equally represented, has been authorised by directives from the chief education officer.

There is no additional regulation of the use of the regional language in the administration or in local authorities. However, it is customary for use of the Alsatian dialect to be permitted in debates in communal assemblies. A decision given by the Colmar court of appeal in 1993 also endorsed the use of Alsatian at the deliberations of a general meeting of members of a private company. There are no regulations governing the use of the Alsatian dialect or German on notices or public signs. However policing powers have been used in the past to discourage the use of these languages in this context. A constitutional reform of 25 June 1992, inserting a provision into article 2 of the Constitution stating that French is the language of the Republic, could now give rise to new problems. According to commentators and positions adopted by the courts, this reform has not affected the validity of local laws drafted in German; (indeed, French translations are for information only; in the event of a dispute, only the original German text is deemed to be authentic). An Act of 4 August 1994 on the use of the French language, superseding an Act of 31 December 1975 on the use of the French language, stipulates a number of legal obligations concerning the use of French. Under the terms of this Act, use of the French language is compulsory in descriptions, offers or displays, written or oral publicity, instructions for use and the scope and terms of guarantees in respect of goods or services, and also in invoices and receipts. The Act does, however, make provision for the use of the regional languages of France. The question is whether in Alsace German is likely to be regarded as a regional language. This is an interpretation frequently put forward in Alsace today.

Although very few provisions under local law could be considered to be an expression of the Alsatian cultural identity, this law has nevertheless increasingly been seen as being representative of the community, making it the genuine expression of a certain Alsatian character. It is true that in itself it somehow reflects the troubled history of Alsace and Lorraine and in this respect contains a true regional cultural dimension. In fact, very few elements of local law justify such an assessment. One could even say that in some respects it is nothing more than an "ersatz" for a genuine regional autonomy which it was not possible to maintain. However, it is not altogether mistaken to see in this regional law a source of local power. Indeed, in view of the aura of mystery which surrounds many local regulations, it is only local experts in this law who are actually able to make use of it, with the result that it is almost impossible to administer it without the active participation of representatives of the local population.

In another connection, local law is also seen as the expression of a particular way of thinking, a specific social order and regional ethical values. In this respect any discussion of local law encompasses the theme of regional consensus. The values expressed in this law are deemed to be both the evidence and instruments of such consensus. The consensual, "corporatist" or administrative features of the provisions which make up local law often contrast with a more bipolar approach, ie an approach influenced by the opposition of divergent interests which is characteristic of French law.

One is also aware of a moral or religious dimension in local law, over and above provisions governing religious affairs. It was through a desire to protect these local ecclesiastical arrangements that other provisions of local law, such as the those governing clubs and associations which had at times been threatened with extinction, were saved. There is no doubt that local law in general has felt the effects of contamination by local ecclesiastical law, with the issue of maintaining the Concordat being seen by the population of Alsace not as a simple religious matter but as threatening its identity or even its very being. This is why many Alsatians consider local law to be a more or less inseparable whole, despite its lack of unity and disparate nature.

B.   *Rules governing the co-existence of local law and general law*

As we have seen local law affects only part, and a very limited part, of the law applicable in Alsace-Moselle. The result is that two bodies of law co-exist in the three *départements* of Eastern France.

The rules governing the co-existence of local law with the laws of the remainder of France, known as general law, have come into existence over time, because local law was originally seen as a temporary phenomenon and so in the beginning no consideration was given to the problems of combining two bodies of law in one State.

The principles for combining them have been arrived at with the aid of the writings of legal scholars and case-law, with certain basic principles being contained in an Act of 24 July 1921 relating to conflicts between civil legislation and local civil legislation and in the two Acts cited earlier of 1 June 1924 concerning the introduction of civil and commercial legislation.

The courts have accepted that all laws "inherently associated with French sovereignty", that is to say those which are intimately connected with the administration of the public authorities and which reflect essential aspects of the French legal system, are automatically applicable throughout the entire national territory. This includes constitutional law and general principles of law.

There is a requirement for other French legislation to have been "introduced" into the recovered territories. Pre-1918 laws must be expressly introduced, but the introduction may cover a whole batch of legislation. For instance, in 1919 two decrees of 25 November 1919 introduced the entire body of French criminal legislation, with a few listed exceptions. This led to problems concerning the definition of "criminal law". Problems have also arisen in determining which authorities have competence to introduce French law into the recovered territories.

For "new" laws, by which we mean post-1918 laws, views have varied regarding the principles governing their introduction into Alsace-Moselle. It could be said that legislation concerning genuinely new subject-matter which does not, as a result, compete with local law, is automatically applicable from the start throughout national territory, except where expressly provided for to the contrary. However, when a new law contradicts a rule of local law, it is considered that the lawmaker must have expressed a desire to repeal the local law and extend the new law to the three *départements* of Eastern France.

Requirements concerning this expression of intention used to be quite strict, but nowadays the revoking of such laws is frequently implicit, it being assumed that, in the absence of a specific exception, the lawmaker wishes the new legislation to apply in the whole of metropolitan France. Consequently, it can be said that today all new legislation is applied "de plano" in Alsace-Moselle, except where the principle is applied whereby the special law (that is, the local law) differs from the general law or where the lawmaker makes a specific exception.

The scope of such local legislation as remains in force may be territorial or personal, as the case may be. The general rule is that local law applies in the territory of Alsace-Moselle. However the scope of some regulations is personal and applies to natives of Alsace-Lorraine wherever they reside in the national territory. These personal regulations concern mainly local legislation with regard to civil status (nationality, legal capacity, matrimonial property regime, etc.). The majority have now been abolished, which facilitates the application of this law, because it was difficult to guarantee the proper application of local law by courts outside the three *départements* of Eastern France.

IV.   Present-day problems with local law in Alsace-Moselle and prospects for the future

As we have seen, local law has not been deliberately constructed on the basis of a theoretical model. It is the result of a pragmatic and flexible reaction to unusual situations. Not being the product of a carefully-conceived political plan, it suffers a number of inconsistencies which affect its practical application and cast doubt on its future.

A.   *Problems with the application of local law in Alsace-Moselle*

The situation whereby specific legislation for Alsace-Moselle is maintained in force, originally intended to be temporary, has now obtained for almost 80 years. Clearly it creates a problem concerning "the management of local law" which manifests itself in a number of ways.

One fundamental issue is how to adapt local legislation to change (whether by repealing, modifying, modernising, etc.). With some exceptions, this is the responsibility of the lawmaker and the national regulatory authorities: local legislation is national legislation with a limited geographical application. Only the regulatory authorities for the ordinary law can change it. The local authorities of Alsace-Moselle therefore have no competence in the matter and do not even need to be consulted.

This situation is explained by the fact that the national authorities did not intend Alsace-Moselle to have autonomous status, but simply to maintain certain local regulations temporarily in force.

In all areas, the law today is an instrument of social change and public action. Maintaining local law in a "crystallised" form is consequently harmful to Alsace-Moselle. Yet the lawmaker and the regulatory authorities are very reluctant to reform local law: beyond objections of principle and a certain hostility to the concept of a specific law, which is inconsistent with the principle of unity, the workload of government and legislature leaves little time for reforming regulations specific to Alsace-Moselle. Anxious not to touch upon sensitive spots, the national regulatory authorities shrink from modifying local laws without first achieving a general consensus at local level. Such agreement is, however, not easily achieved. Finally, the central authorities are ill-equipped to have an adequate knowledge of local law and reform it with sufficient technical expertise.

The result is that local law, which ought to be an asset for the region, tends at times to be a millstone around its neck, an archaic construction which is difficult to set in motion and is ill-suited to present conditions. One might think that this is just what the supporters of a uniform legal system are seeking: in this way they face the supporters of a more regionalised legal system with the dilemma either of conserving provisions which are obsolete, or of abandoning local legislation. In fact, it is the latter which occurs most frequently: many local regulations have become obsolete through non-user, anachronism or <u>de facto</u> abandonment or have simply been forgotten.

In other cases, however, provisions contained in local legislation have so impressed the legislator or the national regulatory authority that they have incorporated it into national legislation, thus achieving the unification of legislation. In this way, acknowledgement of the superiority of local law also leads to its disappearance, when the principles it contains are extended to the rest of France. There are many cases where solutions contained in or inspired by local law have been incorporated into new French law (company law, control of communes, civil procedure, social security, etc), with the result that the superiority of local law has been progressively eroded as the general law has "caught up" with it.

Other problems are associated with the fact that it is sometimes difficult to have knowledge of local legislation: stemming from ancient laws, rarely codified or commented upon and frequently inaccurately translated, local law is not always easy to locate. This is why an "Institute for the local law of Alsace-Moselle" was created in 1985. Involving the public authorities, the legal profession and regional bodies, this is a documentation and research centre which helps to solve most of the problems associated with access or knowledge.

However this body is not always able to give a definitive answer because, in a number of areas, the issue of applicable law is not clear: has the local law remained in force or has it been tacitly abolished? If it has remained in force, what practical application rule arises from its combination with general law? These problems often give rise to issues which fascinate the legal researcher but infuriate the practitioner.

B.   Prospects for the future

Problems such as these have not turned the inhabitants of Alsace-Moselle against their local laws. According to recent surveys, the inhabitants of Alsace and Moselle are attached to their local legislation and want to keep it. 82% believe that it is very good or quite good and 89% believe that the existence of local law is good for Alsace-Moselle. Only 3% think it should be abolished. Obviously, the most favourable opinions concern additional holidays based on local law and the local complementary health insurance scheme. However, even with regard to the local religious arrangements, vigorously opposed by "secular" groups, only 9% of the population would like to see these abolished.

So what are the prospects for the future of the local laws of Alsace-Moselle? In reality, this depends on how the French institutional system develops. If it remains fixed on its present line of uniform and monolithic development, the local law of Alsace-Moselle will become increasingly archaic and marginalised. If, on the other hand, under the combined influence of "globalisation" and European integration, France seeks to revitalise and reinforce the traditions of plurality and diversity which are as much a part of its identity as the Jacobin tradition, then local laws may be redeployed and used, if not as a model, at least in an experimental capacity.

The prospects for such developments today appear to be quite limited. But France is capable of rapid and unexpected change. The decentralisation which was set in motion in 1982 had a profound effect on territorial organisation. France's decision to work towards European integration has already had radical consequences on relations between the government and the economy. In the areas of law and public institutions, changes which are unthinkable today will be unavoidable tomorrow.

However another problem stems from the great reluctance of the people of Alsace and Lorraine to express their wishes in this area. It may be thought that the majority of this population would be in favour of extending regionalisation, already widely embarked upon, to local law. However, the "frontier" nature of this region does nothing to encourage such a demand, which might easily be discredited as "separatist". Consequently neither local nor regional authorities, nor representative political groups have made any formal demand for a redefinition of local law.

It is possible, however, to outline the possible terms of such a redefinition. Two changes would be required to transform local laws into a genuine territorial code:
-the "repatriation" of local legislation: we have seen that this is national legislation with limited geographical application. In order to regionalise this local legislation, it would be necessary to give regional or local organs direct or indirect regulatory powers. This could be achieved, for example, by adopting legislation delegating the power to change local laws to local organs. This already exists in some areas where the law merely establishes a framework which the local authorities are responsible for putting into effect (for example, with regard to the regulations for Sunday and public holiday closing for shops). In reality this would be a transfer of regulatory powers to local authorities. The participation of regional or local authorities in the enactment or transformation of regulations with regional scope could also take the form of a mechanism for the systematic consultation of these authorities by central regulatory bodies, as is already provided for by the set of laws governing Corsica or the Overseas *départements* and Territories: before enacting regulations specific to these regions, parliament or government consults with their representative organs.

- the "redeployment" of local legislation: we have seen that some regulations under local law only survive because of their function as "ersatz" for a genuine status of territorial autonomy. Because they are unable to express an opinion in areas of interest to them, local populations cling to regulations with no real interest, but which enable them to express in a "symbolic" manner, however inadequate, their wish to protect their regional identity. If they were permitted to express this identity in areas which are dear to them and where there are real particularities to be taken into account, it would be possible to persuade them to abandon local laws which were merely "parasitic". It would then be necessary to refocus local legislation on areas where it would have genuine regional cultural, social or institutional significance. Certain curiosities of the law of divisions of communes or of local civil procedure could then be abandoned in favour of a real status for the regional language or a specific organisation for Alsace-Moselle territorial authorities.

Areas on which such refocused local legislation ought to be concentrated include: education, language, regional audiovisual media, culture, the protection of nature, trans-frontier cooperation and local democracy. With regard to this last item, it is increasingly accepted that the ordinary territorial structure which exists in France today (region and *départements*) is not appropriate in a small region such as Alsace; a different distribution of powers within the region would therefore be desirable. Local legislation would be maintained, albeit in a modernised and regionalised form, where it concerns religious activities, apprenticeships, craft trades and hunting, since these are of considerable regional cultural relevance. The social aspects (local administration and social security, Sunday rest days and public holidays, social assistance) would also be worth conserving in a modernised form, as would a number of technical regulations which do not pose any particular problems (notification of information relating to real estate, etc).

*

*　　　　*

A reorganisation of the legal system of Alsace-Moselle along these lines, leading to a specific territorial status, could contribute to the overall development of the institutional system in France into a pluralist and more regionalised organisation.

FRIDAY 25 OCTOBER 1996

Mr Giancarlo CRUDER,
President of the Regional Council of Friuli-Venezia-Giulia

Excellencies, Ladies and Gentlemen

It falls to me, as President of the Regional Council of Friuli-Venezia-Giulia to open and coordinate the work of today's morning session of the Conference on Federalism, Regionalism, Local Self-Government and Minorities organised by the Council of Europe in conjunction with the Region.

By way of introduction, and before giving the floor to the speakers, I would like to express my special gratitude to the officers of the Standing Conference of Local and Regional Authorities, a constituent body of the Council of Europe, for choosing this region and this city as the venue for this discussion, because in these lands, lying in a border zone - borders which have for many decades been a dividing curtain between two separate worlds -the problem of minorities and their treatment has always been an outstanding and serious political problem.

It is a well known fact that here we have a minority linguistic and national tradition, Slovenian, which is related to the language, history and traditions of the neighbouring Republic of Slovenia and which demands a special role and status to safeguard its own ethnic and cultural characteristics and its own identity.

But Friuli-Venezia-Giulia also has the characteristics of a regional community, in which the Friulian language and culture are an essential component of the ethnic and cultural identity of its people and the protection of this is a central issue in the development of the special form of self-government granted to the Region.

The mature sensitivity by which we live and work in these lands, by which the aspirations for recognition of their linguistic and cultural diversity present must be politically interpreted, in these circumstances has the opportunity to find expression and manifest itself through a full understanding of the problem which we are to analyze and an outline of the choices made up to now to meet these requirements for care and development of the minorities.

In Friuli-Venezia-Giulia - a meeting point for three cultures and three lands situated right at the heart of complex international events - there has long been an awareness of the significance and the value of minorities and the need to protect them properly.

These, far from representing a reason for weakening the community, must be made a means of enriching it, not just culturally but economically, joining three different worlds, a precious instrument for economic interaction.

Thus it is that, in this way, minorities can really begin to make a significant contribution to building a Europe based on the principles of democracy and respect for diversity, and their development and protection can be a force for promoting neighbourly living and the common good.

The Friuli-Venezia-Giulia Region, albeit within the limits of its competence, has sought, in its activities, to make an effective contribution in respect of the needs for protection of the Slovenian minority.

Given that responsibility for protection primarily belongs to the State, it has now, in the areas and matters within its ambit, introduced legislation to support those belonging to the minority group which has extended the safeguard arrangements in their favour.

As far as safeguarding the Friulian linguistic and cultural heritage is concerned, - in addition to many measures taken in the past - an organic law was recently passed which allows the Region itself to pursue an active policy for preserving and developing that language and culture so as to preserve its characteristics and identity.

Precisely because of this mature awareness of the needs of minority groups, there is hope and expectation that the needs of the Italian national group which today lives separately in districts of Slovenia and Croatia - and which are relevant to this Region -can be properly taken into account by recognising a homogeneous treatment which consolidates the single identity and character.

The initiatives that even now may be in progress for that minority seem to open up reassuring glimmers of light, and this is very much welcomed.

The problem that is certainly now raised with great urgency - and this is the discussion that the Conference has sought to address - is which systems of self-government are best suited to ensuring effective safeguard arrangements for ethnic, cultural and linguistic differences within a single jurisdiction.

There is currently a great and lively debate in Italy and the Italian Regions on what form of State to choose, what solutions to adopt - whether a confederal regionalism or centrally imposed federal system - to meet the challenge of greater efficiency in government action and greater "closeness" of institutions to the problems of the people. In other words, how to make better application of the principle of subsidiarity.

The confrontation is right out in the open. The regions themselves have put forward their proposal for a federal structure of the State, based on full recognition of the fundamental functions which can be carried out by the institutions in closest direct contact with social realities, primarily the local authorities and regions themselves. It is a proposal which was recently taken on board by the Regional Council of Friuli-Venezia-Giulia, as a direction for legislative activity.

It is in this context, which concerns both the means and effectiveness of moving institutional structures closer to the communities real problems, that the role of safeguarding minorities will be reserved to regional and local bodies.

Even today, article 6 of the Italian Constitution provides for the participation of all levels of government institutions in protecting minorities.

But the way that article is applied and its narrow interpretation have not so far allowed a wholly satisfactory collaboration between State and regional legislation in defining safeguard policies.

In today's Italian legislation, minorities are protected more by virtue of special laws adopted with constituting statutes or on the basis of international standards than under article 6 of the Constitution.

There has not been up to now a serious and in-depth effort to achieve protection of minorities defined in general terms in relation to the provisions of the Constitution. Thus, many of the contributions have only been achieved through jurisprudence, in the absence of precise legislation and choices by the national legislator.

In this context, however, regional legislation has been growing in importance, and this has now led to a broader concept of minorities and thus to a lowering of the level of protection.

It thus seems appropriate that in redesigning the institutional structure of the Italian State - although the issue is becoming of general concern involving all the countries of Europe - the issue of minorities should only be considered in order to define the degree of intervention by the State legislator, regional and local government so as to ensure different types of protection relevant to the specific diversities in an area, based, however, on certain general principles which are protected and respected.

This need certainly focuses on the fundamental task, on which all must be agreed, to continue and then develop the process of European integration, in which the rights of all minorities to their own ethnic and linguistic identity, and full participation in economic, social and political life must be recognised and protected.

The dramas of the past, and the no less dramatic events which we have only recently witnessed because of the rekindling of the nationalist flame and xenophobic madness must never again be repeated and must give way to broader understanding between peoples, each the bearer of their own history, culture, language and traditions which are respected and protected.

The implications of the problem which we are facing are of no little account. It is not just a matter of institutional engineering, but of the political will to accept fully and put into practice the principles of democracy and respect for individuals and groups, by which we are all under the obligation to build a common European home.

We have before us a challenging road, but the way has already been pointed.

The presence of many representatives of member countries of the Council of Europe in this Conference is a great testimony to the will explore these questions more deeply together, so as to find solutions which can provide all our minorities with that just protection through full respect for the rights of individuals and groups, which no democracy can fail to recognize and protect if it really wants to be a democracy.

Prof. Gilberto PRESSACCO,
Conservatorio Tomadini, Udine (italy)

Minorities and Regional Autonomy: regions holding a special status in italy

1. The previous situation under the Italian Constitution
2. Minorities and the 1948 Italian Constitution
3. Federalism and the pluralistic organisation of the state

1. The previous situation under the Italian Constitution

Protection of minorities in the modern sense started with the preparation of legal instruments intended to allow exceptions to the "cuius regio eius et religio" principle. The 1606 Treaty of Vienna between Hungary and the Prince of Transylvania gave members of the Transylvanian protestant minority the right freely to practise their protestant faith. Other examples followed during the seventeenth century, typical among these being the 1648 Treaty of Westphalia, which marked the beginning of the history of nation-states (superiorem non recognoscentes). And it is still along the same line of the affirmation of the national principle that the nineteenth century extended the protection of minorities from the religious to the ethnic/linguistic. The first thing to be said about this development is that, on the one hand, the regulations covering states with more than one ethnic group and/or language are placed in the same category (eg the Austrian Constitution of 1867 and the Swiss Constitution of 1874), and, on the other, there is another category for treaties between states which offered reciprocal protection to their own minorities, where it was impossible to place "national minorities" within the limits of the "motherland". The high point of this effort came in the League of Nations, in the aftermath of World War I, and this is reflected in the obligations vis-à-vis minorities imposed by the victorious states in the peace treaties with Austria, Bulgaria, Hungary and Turkey.

This system was swept away with the advent of fascism in Europe. Following World War II, the main trend which emerged was one of the protection of individuals' rights, rather than the rights of minority groups as such. It is indeed significant that the United Nations Charter (San Francisco, 1944) contains no provisions for the benefit of minority groups. The General Assembly merely approved an agenda which made it clear that the UN could not fail to take an interest in the fate of minorities. This approach probably stemmed from the emphasis placed by the Anglo-American culture on individual rights, but also represented the UN's distancing itself from the nation-state situation, which had brought more than a few problems with it. Individual protection, expressed mainly in the form of non-discrimination, radically reduced the profile of the issue of minorities as a group. Even against this background, however, there was no shortage of international treaties for the protection of minorities, such as, in the case of Italy, the De Gasperi-Grüber agreement on Alto Adige/South Tyrol (1946) and the special status for Trieste in an appendix to the London Memorandum (1954).

A new cultural climate subsequently developed, leading to the restoration of minority protection as a political and social value. The logic of protection is now a matter for social pluralism, by which is meant society's relationship with all the different experiences of human beings. It is this new atmosphere that has given rise to legal texts such as Article 14 of the European Convention on Human Rights and Article 27 of the UN's International Covenant on Civil and Political Rights (1966), as well as texts offering guidance, such as the Council of Europe's European Charter for Regional or Minority Languages (1992).

2.   Minorities and the 1948 Italian Constitution

Between 1861 and 1918, national concerns overshadowed any possible consideration of minorities. Suffice it to say that the scope of the rules of the Kingdom of Piedmont protecting the use of the French language in the French-speaking valleys such as the Valle d'Aosta was even reduced (yet French was the language of the ruling house!). In this general atmosphere, things were certainly no better for the Slovenes of the Natisone valleys, which became part of the Kingdom of Italy in 1866, or for the other groups of minority language-speakers scattered in various parts of Italy. Thus it came about (as described by Pizzorusso, one of the greatest experts in Italian constitutional law on this subject) that the linguistic differences between Sardinians and Friulians were reduced to mere dialect variants of Italian.

After World War I, when Istria and South Tyrol became part of Italy, the situation demanded a climate of tolerance, at least, and all the more so for the fact that the League of Nations had devised a policy for the protection of minorities.

Then the atmosphere changed, a typical case being that of the most closely-knit minority, the South Tyroleans, who in 1939 were encouraged to opt for incorporation in Germany in the framework of the agreements between Hitler and Mussolini.

Following World War II, the problem raised its head again. The case of the French-speaking group in the Valle d'Aosta was resolved through internal legislation, a large measure of self-government being granted to the Valle d'Aosta, but it should not be forgotten that the issue gave rise to much discussion in the Resistance itself, and that it was the strong personality of the historian and politician, Federico Chabod, which won the day and earned broad recognition from Italy.

The German case, in contrast, weighed heavily on the peace conference, the focus being on the De Gasperi-Grüber agreement appended to the peace treaty. It was, however, not easy to put the agreement into practice. The problem of the Slovenes, parallel to that of the Italians in Istria, was subject to more than a few conditions as a result of the events connected with the border with former Yugoslavia. No organic solution to the Slovene problem has yet been found, since the protection rules are those in the appendix to the London Memorandum on the definition of what is known as the Free Territory of Trieste and in certain regulations covering schools approved by central government and on cultural affairs approved by the Friuli-Venezia-Giulia Region.

Up to this point, the issue of "ethnic/national and linguistic minorities" may be said to have been tackled through international legal offices (the Germans of Alto Adige and the Slovenes of Friuli-Venezia-Giulia) or through quasi-international legal offices (the French of the Valle d'Aosta). The issue of the protection of the respective minorities dates from the nineteenth century. The inclusion of Article 6 ("The Republic safeguards linguistic minorities by means of special provisions") of the Italian Constitution opened the Italian system to the new pluralist concept. This it achieved, but not unambiguously. On the one hand a large number of members of the Constituent Assemblies wished to avoid such explicit rules, taking the view that the problem would be solved through the creation of

60

Regions with special status, and also interpreting the rules concerned exclusively within the problem area of national linguistic minorities.

This is confirmed by the objective fact that, even after serious efforts first to investigate the technical/cultural aspects, and then to move legislation (mainly at the initiative of Friulian MPs), the Italian Parliament as a body has never succeeded in passing outline rules covering all of Italy's linguistic minorities. And it has to be said that, apart from some praiseworthy exceptions, neither Italian culture in general, nor Italy's legal circles in particular, have supported any such operations of political and legal civilisation.

So we are a long way from the full development in this area of one of the cardinal principles of the 1948 Constitution, that of pluralism. Article 6 of the Constitution would systematically be taken in conjunction with Article 2 ("The Republic recognizes and guarantees the inviolable rights of man, both as an individual and as a member of the social groups in which his personality finds expression, ...") and with the second sub-paragraph of Article 3 ("It is the responsibility of the Republic to remove all obstacles of an economic and social nature which, by limiting the freedom and equality of citizens, prevent the full development of the individual and the participation of all workers in the political, economic and social organization of the country").

Even the Statute of Friuli-Venezia-Giulia, approved by Constitutional Law No 1 of 1963, does not manage to bring this concept to fruition: Article 3 merely confirms the principle of negative protection in the form of non-discrimination (stating that, in Regions, parity of rights and treatment for all citizens shall be recognised, whatever the linguistic group to which they belong, with safeguards for respective ethnic and cultural characteristics). This reference to the safeguarding of ethnic and cultural characteristics not only was weak from the outset, but also can be described as having failed in practice to provide significant pointers to minority policy.

3.   Federalism and the pluralistic organisation of the state

It is reasonable to wonder whether this outcome of minority policy was taken for granted from the start of the Republic. The Italian Constitution, although it takes an ambiguous approach to the question, actually had potential in this field, but this was not explored, with both culture and politics swinging to and fro between national concerns and the individualistic process of gaining freedom. The pluralist factor, in the communities, was in practice eclipsed.

Yet it cannot be denied that the wording "The Republic safeguards..." means that all the republic's authorities (ie central government, regions, provinces and municipalities) are involved in various ways in the protection process. The wording of Article 5 ("The Republic, which is one and indivisible, recognizes and promotes local autonomy; it applies the fullest measure of administrative decentralization in services dependent on the State and adjusts the principles and methods of its legislation to the requirements of autonomy and decentralization") undeniably signifies that both central government and sub-national authorities have dealings with a great variety of groups and individuals.

Yet it was not until local government reform in 1990, following the ending of statutory self-government, and thus of the possibility of including the relevant principle in national legislation, that the question of Italy's ethnic and linguistic pluralism was able to be raised again in municipal and provincial Statutes. Nothing similar happened, moreover, when Regions were created in Italy, nor when public administration was reformed. Even the school system shows the effects of centralised management: the curriculum instructions to adapt humanities studies to the local situation were frustrated, despite being included in a series of provisions subsequent to secondary school reform, and school staffing policy is completely inappropriate for striking the right balance between local cultures and languages and the mass schooling system. It is to be hoped that some fresh impetus will come from the new faculty of arts/education sciences.

Thus the subjects to the fore during the unification of the country are again part of Italy's debate on state reform. There is discussion not only of the form of government, but also of the form of the state.

The search for the answer has brought growing interest in some form of strong regionalism, not yet existent, but verging on the federal development of the Italian state.

The historical/natural regions, on which the Constituent Assemblies of 1946/48 based their work, still seem to be the necessary reference points during discussions of Italian regionalism. In fact, constitutions, in order to avoid being pure tools of institutional engineering, have to try to provide an appropriate legal framework for the communities, and not force communities into a theory-based straitjacket. Another question, to which a different solution may be found, is that of the institutions' efficiency. Forms of institutionalised co-operation between Regions can cope with this problem.

The issue of ethnic/linguistic minorities will certainly be able to be resolved in this new institutional framework, thus finally emerging from the "bilateral protection" system, which always implies dependence on the nationality principle, ultimately moving towards full implementation of the pluralist principle.

In an institutional system which distributes specific powers to each tier, it is logical for an institutional solution also to be found for the problem of ethnic/linguistic minorities. This is the only way of putting fully into practice the principle laid down in Article 6 of the present Constitution, the principle that every institutional level is to play its part in the protection of minorities. It will thus be better to refer to a pluralist organisation of the Italian system, rather than to the protection of minorities. Nor can the school system fail to be reviewed in the light of this approach (what is more, this subject has already been looked at from precisely this angle during the discussion of the system most appropriate for the united Italy).

The European Union certainly provides an excellent framework now for serious consideration and for a positive resolution of this problem. The discussions come at the end of a long period of history which we can date back to the sixteenth century, and their importance will not be negligible when we come to appraise the quality of the future.

Mr José María MUÑOA GANUZA,
Deputy to the President of the Basque Government (Spain)
with responsibility for foreign relations

Regional autonomy: the autonomous status of the Basque Country

Mr President,
Ladies and Gentlemen,
Dear Friends,

It is both an honour and a pleasure for me to address you today, you who are experts in your field and who represent the member States of the Council of Europe, in order to describe the Basque country's real political and institutional situation and its relations with Spanish central government and the European Union.

Therefore I first wish to thank you for having given me the floor at such an exceptional, prestigious gathering.

It is a well-known fact that the political and philosophical ideas based on Jacobinism and the concept of the centralised nation-state that spread through 19th-century Europe had a far-reaching influence on Spain and in the end shook the country's *ancien régime* to its foundations.

However, it is less well known that this influence did not enable the territorial integration to which some parties aspired.

This is why in Spain the concept of the State is far less synonymous with that of the nation than in other countries, with the result that I consider myself a Basque by nationality but a citizen of the Kingdom of Spain, a point of view which it is difficult for people elsewhere to understand and accept.

The aim of bringing the two concepts, or even better the two realities, into convergence has periodically exerted an impact on Spanish politics in the course of the past two centuries.

It would be a denial of the historical truth if I failed to point out that Spain's attempts merely to copy a centralised form of State with very different historical and sociological origins almost always involved the use of force; this persistently led to unsatisfactory situations, in which violence was moreover a dominant factor.

However, it should be said that the last serious attempt, which could have a lasting effect if it is pursued with even greater care and realism, was made at the time of the recent democratisation process, which led to approval of a new Constitution in 1978 and to the Basque Country's Statute of Autonomy in 1979.

Spain's most recent Constitution clearly takes the option, once again, of identifying the State with the nation. However, the authors were obliged to pay heed to the true state of affairs and to introduce a third concept - difficult to transpose into legal or political terms - for which they adopted the expression "nationality" or "historical nationality".

They thus attempted to allow for - but not expressly recognise - the historical distinction we make between the State and the nation.

Hence two politically different trends came together in the Spanish Constitution of 1978, and it was subsequently often tried to make an amalgam of them.

Firstly, the Constitution instituted or developed a new territorial organisation based on decentralisation of power, known as the State of Autonomies.

Secondly, it acknowledged, approved and updated the status as political entities of a number of specific territories and took that status into consideration in defining the powers of these self-governing communities.

In the case of the Basque Country these two constitutional developments - recognition and decentralisation - merge perfectly and complement each other in so far as the region's historical rights are henceforth guaranteed by the Constitution.

This merger of the two trends is far from being a mere matter of rhetoric or of reference to the past since it has clear legal and political consequences for the Basque Country and its self-government.

One of these consequences, which is widely accepted, relates to the components of its autonomy, that is to say the range of powers which it enjoys. Another consequence, which is still disputed, relates to how those powers are exercised, or in other words the kind of relationship that has to be established between central government and the institutions of the Autonomous Community of the Basque Country.

On the subject of the components of self-government, I merely wish to say that, as with the other Autonomous Communities, the Statute of Autonomy gives the Basque Country authority for all levels of education, health, social services, culture, housing, town and country planning, transport and communication infrastructure, local election law and many other matters of major social and economic significance.

However, in addition, by virtue of the Constitution's recognition of its historical nationality, the Autonomous Community of the Basque Country enjoys complete independence in other spheres, and I wish to draw your attention to two of the most important of them.

The first is that of law enforcement. The Ertzaintza, the autonomous Basque police force, has its origins in the traditional forces formed in the past and is responsible for almost all law-enforcement duties since only matters of a supra- or extra-Community nature lie outside its jurisdiction. I am sure that you will have read in the press of this 7,500-member police force's efficiency in bringing the perpetrators of certain offences before the courts.

The second specific power, which is exercised by the "Foral" Community of Navarra for the same historical reasons, is that of taxation, recovery of taxes and finance.

In co-operation with central government, the Autonomous Community has authority to regulate tax matters and to collect all taxes within its territory, including taxes on monopolies but excluding customs duties. We collect personal income tax, corporation tax, VAT, and so on, and of course local taxes. We also have discretion to fix the rates of most of these taxes. In short, we are to all intents and purposes granted the resources of any Ministry of Finance.

This exceptional authority naturally results in a special relationship with the State.

Whereas in most systems, even those that are decentralised, central government usually collects taxes and passes on to the territorial authorities the resources needed to run the services they manage, in the Basque Country the opposite applies. After agreeing with the State on the cost of a given sphere - the armed forces, foreign policy, the royal family - for which the State assumes authority on its behalf, the Basque Country pays a contribution, which is also jointly agreed upon, to this general expense. This state of affairs has two important consequences.

Firstly, the Autonomous Community of the Basque Country enjoys considerable independence in managing its own resources and defining its own priorities, a situation which involves certain risks and responsibilities.

Secondly, this relationship between the State and the Autonomous Community bears a closer resemblance to federalism than to any other system of government.

At this point in my address I therefore wish to emphasise that the Basque Country is a special, separate case within the Kingdom of Spain, and for that very reason a complex one.

Both the Basque Country's originality and the complexity this entails in its relationship with the State remain politically controversial issues today. The 1978 Constitution was highly ambiguous and allowed wide scope for flexibility on the subject of autonomy. The intention was that this flexibility would enable a gradual, realistic response to the State's territorial diversity and the particularities of its "different nationalities". Time has shown that, on the contrary, ambiguity and flexibility can also be used by those who take a neo-centrist, pro-standardisation stance to bring pressure to bear on how the Constitution is interpreted.

However, this is a matter of hard facts and the worst course of action would be to ignore them or to pretend they did not exist. In the case of Spain, it is a source of error to seek obstinately and unnecessarily to copy the models of other States when Spain has never reached the same degree of territorial organisation or national integration.

Spanish territorial organisation is what it is - no better nor worse than any other, but simply different and it is Spain's alone. It is an organisation within which strong national sentiments co-exist, but these are not synonymous with a sense of belonging to a single State or, if you prefer, a sense of shared citizenship. Given this state of affairs, only acceptance and separate promotion of these two feelings - and one's dominance over the other - make possible further progress with the form of territorial organisation - involving both advantages and disadvantages - which has evolved in the course of Spain's history.

There can be no doubt that the Spanish Constitution is a serious attempt to move in that direction. Although we Basque nationalists abstained from approving it, because we regarded it as inadequate, we acknowledge that an effort was made to recognise the existence of "nationalities" within the Kingdom of Spain and to safeguard and modernise our "historical rights". In this respect the Constitution deserved our full respect and opened up a path which was worth taking. But in the end it was what I initially referred to as a "constitutional loophole" that enabled we democratic Basque nationalists to move resolutely and full of hope towards statutory recognition of the co-existence of what we regard as the Basque nation within the Kingdom of Spain.

In sum, the Basque Country can find a place for itself in a Spanish State with a complex, asymmetrical structure, showing regard for differences and personalities, in a State at peace with its history and its own form of territorial organisation and hence ready to disregard the constant temptation to standardise and to adopt instead an attitude more in tune with reality. Such a State would be the outcome of a reasonable, responsible interpretation of the 1978 Constitution and the Basque Country's Statute of Autonomy of 1979.

Yet at the same time as it carves out a place for itself within a complex State our Autonomous Community must face the consequences of Spain's membership of the European Community and the changes the Community has undergone to date.

We Basques have always perceived Europe as the most propitious environment for the development of our personality and self-government. This point of view is based, in our case, on the situation as it stands and on our own hopes.

The Spanish government and the Basque government have already formed a bilateral committee, which will be used, among other things, to establish a joint position as to the State's intentions vis-à-vis the European Union on matters coming within our jurisdiction, and we do not, after all, rule out the possibility of opening up direct channels of communication and representation with Community institutions in order to defend our own interests.

I believe certain local or regional entities, including our own, have already shown sufficient proof of their realistic, responsible attitudes for those who sincerely want European economic and political union to consider them as genuine and efficient partners.

It does not have to be said here that the European "regional" movement includes entities with very different legal, political and social personalities. The role each of them assumes within Europe will therefore depend on the status they enjoy, whether now or in future, within their own State. It would not be realistic, as things stand at present, to imagine the European Union giving the same functions to regions whose status within their respective States is very different. The States themselves will therefore be the first to discriminate.

This is tantamount to saying that the "regional" movement does not call into question the States' own, exclusive role in European integration. The aim is therefore not to replace them but to re-balance the situation. We are aware that the European Union is at present, and for some time, founded on the corner-stones which its member States represent.

However, having acknowledged that fact, we also believe that the nature of the State and the thinking of those who directly manage its principal spheres of authority - defence, foreign policy and the economic and monetary system - still embody something which, when the time comes, prevents the step needed to form a genuine European Union from being taken. It is against this background that the Community institutions and all those who sincerely desire European unity can find support and assistance among certain local and regional authorities, in particular those with a strong political personality.

We also believe that, at a time when the present European States are accused of having been unable to inspire confidence in their citizens and having acted in a furtive, remote fashion, our readiness to assume the role of a mediator in favour of increased European awareness may be a valuable asset to those who are striving to achieve the ideal of a truly united Europe.

If I were asked to describe a European Union in which nationality, such as the Basque nationality, would easily be accommodated, I would not hesitate to propose a Union that should combine more of Europe, less of the State, more of the nation and much more society.

More of Europe means more room for shared management of State sovereignty in matters such as defence, foreign policy, the economy, monetary control and social cohesion.

Less of the State means increasingly less room for autonomous management of the traditional spheres of sovereignty mentioned above and also, through widespread application of the subsidiarity principle, less and less room for States to exercise power within their respective territories.

More of the nation means strengthening those entities capable of integrating groups of citizens who are really united by a sense of community, and also of developing competitively viable economic projects on a scale which can be mastered and implementing efficient, controllable systems to provide services to citizens (health, social services, education, urban security).

Lastly, more society means far more European citizenship with direct, efficient means of electing and controlling the institutions that manage the Union. The so-called "democratic deficit" from which those institutions currently suffer must be drastically reduced. In my opinion, on this level attempts to build a Union without at the same time building a European support system, that is without making suitable arrangements for citizens' direct participation in European politics, have been a cause of failure. Yet again, our help will be absolutely essential to build this union.

Ladies and Gentlemen, I have to conclude here. I have tried to draw a picture of what Euskadi is and can become within Spain and within the European Union, but this picture is undoubtedly incomplete and should give rise to a large number of questions.

Prof. Dr. Silvo DEVETAK,
European Centre for Ethnic, Regional and Sociological Studies at
the University of Maribor (Slovenia)

Minorities and autonomy in Central and Eastern European Countries

Minorities in central and eastern Europe are distributed throughout the zone which stretches almost continuously from the Adriatic Sea to the south of Lithuania (excluding the ex-Soviet Union). According to Foucher this area corresponds to former frontier zones and strategic regions which have been, throughout the centuries, places of confrontation, stakes to be fought for and areas in which imperial frontiers were subject to change. This area was constituted by regions with unstable population where the balance of power was a constant issue. These regions were by definition places which were propitious to the endless displacement of ethnic communities [1].

The status of ethnic minorities is to-day a crucial issue at stake in the process of Nation-building, both in old and especially in the newly created states. The greatest threat to the security of many states is thus their internal conflict with different kinds of minorities which is in most cases a consequence of their failure to find strength in diversity. The repression of minorities has been shown to be an unsuccessful strategy fuelling conflicts and retarding development.

It is more and more obvious that new approaches to the resolution of ethnic conflicts and to the regulation of ethnic problems should be studied, especially those concerning the dichotomy between integration and diversity; concerning democracy and decentralisation of power; regulation and functioning of multicultural societies; suppression of nationalism, xenophobia; and concerning different practical new scenarios for protection of minorities [1], dealing for instance with electoral system (local balance representation, communal balance representation) [2], minority veto for changing the constitution [3], and autonomy [4].

---

[1] Michel Foucher, Minorities in central and eastern Europe (1994), Strasbourg, Council of Europe Press, p. 19.

[1] E.K. Francis, Interethnic Relations, New York, Elsevier (1976) pp. 386-429.

[2] See David Chapman, Can Civil War be avoided ? Electoral and Constitutional Models for Ethnically Divided Countries, London, The Institute for Social Inventions (1991), pp. 62-83, 88-90, 146-149.

[3] Arend Lijphart, Democraties, Pattern of Majoritarian and Consensus Government in Twenty-One Countries, New Haven, Yale University Press (1984), pp. 189-190.

[4] See National Separatism, Ed. Collin H. Williams, Cardiff, University of Wales Press (1982), especially pp. 96, 101, 110, 115, 173, 389, 391.

A VARIETY OF MODELS

In theory the terms political, regional, territorial, functional, personal, and cultural autonomy are used in order to specify different ways and means of participation of the members of an ethnic, linguistic, cultural or religious minority in the self-governing of the territory where they live or in managing matters which constitute their separate identity. Some author use the term power sharing in order to explain the participation of minorities in the decision-making processes. Each of these models of autonomy has its own characteristics; in practice all of these types are intermingled and overlapping [5] The term autonomy is derived from Greek: auto means self, nomos is law. Autonomy in the legal-political vocabulary - denotes self-government. The European Charter of Local Self-government defines self-government as "the right and the ability of local authorities, within the limits of the law, to regulate and manage a substantial share of public affairs under their own responsibility and in the interest of the local population" (art.3) [6]. Autonomy means the legal recognition of minorities and minorities rights. It excludes absolute majority rule in view of the special values of a minority. Autonomy is closely connected with human rights [7]. Autonomy arrangements constitute usually a part of a state's system of government.

Normally, the protected minority inhabits a certain part of the state territory. Granting autonomy to an ethnically mixed area allows the people inhabiting it to exercise direct control over important affairs of special concern to them, while allowing the larger entity, which retains certain powers over the area, to exercise those powers which are in the common interest of both entities [8]. In the case we speak of the territorial autonomy which gives an ethnic minority political control over a certain territory. A territorially concentrated ethnic minority can govern its own affairs to a greater or lesser extent, either through devolution of powers or through a federal structure assuring the central government and regional components of designated powers. How extensive those powers are - for instance, regional elective government, command of local police, control over natural resources, management of regional schools - depends upon the bargain reached between a minority and other political forces in the society [9].

The FUEN Draft Convention on the Protection of Ethnic Groups in Europe (art.4) defines a territorial autonomy as a right of ethnic groups forming the majority of the population in the areas where they are settled to "special status within a demarcated territory, denominated territorial autonomy,

---

[5]   For broader information on this topic see Minorities and Autonomy in Western Europe, compiled and edited by Minority Rights Group (Manchester Free Press, London, 1991).

[6]   See European Charter of Local Self-Government, European Treaty Series n° 122 (Council of Europe, Strasbourg, 15 octobre 1985).

[7]   Bernhardt, Rudolf. Federalisme and Autonomy, in Dinstein, Yoram (Ed.), Models of Autonomy (New Brunswick, London, 1981), p. 27.

[8]   Sohn, Louis B.(1981) Models of Autonomy Within the United Nations Framework, in: Dinstein, Yoram (Ed.), Models of Autonomy (New Brunswick - London), p.5.

[9]   Henry J. Steiner (1991), Ideals and Counter-Ideals in the Struggle Over Autonomy Regimes for Minorities, Notre Dame Law Review, 66:1539, p. 1542.

with an autonomous legislation, government, administration and judiciary" [10]. In addition, art.9 defines "local autonomy" as a right of local self-determination of the ethnic groups who are "not forming the majority of the population" as well as of ethnic groups settled in "isolated settlements" [11].

Article 11 of the protocol to the ECHR, proposed by the Recommendation 1201 (1993) of the Parliamentary Assembly of the Council of Europe reads as follows: "In the regions where they are a majority, the persons belonging to national minorities shall have the right to have at their disposal appropriate local or autonomous authorities or to have a special status, matching this specific historical and territorial situation and in accordance with the domestic legislation of the State." [12] This provision is not an operative rule of international law but a mere proposal to which reference is made in bilateral treaties signed between Hungary and Croatia, Slovakia and Romania.

What we call functional autonomy is in fact a model of power-sharing regimes. Such regimes assure ethnic groups of a particular form of participation in governance or in economic opportunities. Members of minorities may be constitutionally entitled to elect a stated percentage of members of the national legislature through the use of separate voting rolls that list competing candidates drawn only from the relevant minority. All legislators who are members of a particular minority may be authorised to vote as a bloc with power to veto proposed measures adversely affecting the minority, such as a change in official languages or voting schemes. Representatives of minorities may be assured of formal consultation by the government projects. Cabinet positions or a certain portion of the judiciary may be reserved for minority groups etc. [13]. Article 14 of the Venice Commission's proposal for the Convention for the Protection of Minorities provides that "States shall favour the effective participation of minorities in public affairs, in particular decisions affecting the regions where they live or the matters affecting them."

Where an ethnic minority is scattered over the whole or the greater part of the state, it is conceivable that there will be "personal" autonomy and not "territorial" [14]. There is the opinion that personal autonomy does not make sense except as a complement to territorial autonomy [15]. The difference between territorial and personal autonomy has been defined in the following terms: territorial autonomy is established in a delineated portion of the territory of a state and it relates to all the inhabitants within the area; personal autonomy is accorded to members of a certain (ethnic, linguistic or religious) community irrespective of their place of residence. This model of autonomy provides that the members of an ethnic community will be governed by a personal law distinctive to it. A personal law can provide an important degree of autonomy and cohesion even for minorities that are territorially dispersed [16]. Article 15 of the Framework Convention on the Rights of National Minorities introduced

---

[10]   Protection of Ethnic Groups in Europe, II, Autonomy Rights of Ethnic Groups in Europe, Discussion Document for a Special Convention, 12 May 1994, p.53

[11]   12 ibid, p.60.

[12]   For the text of the protocol see Council of Europe, Protection of the Rights of Minorities, Doc. 7572, pp. 2-7.

[13]   See Henry J. Steiner, supra note, pp. 1541-42.

[14]   See Bernhardt, supra note, p. 27.

[15]   See Dinstein, Yoram (Ed.), Models of Autonomy (New Brunswick, London, 1981), p. 293.

[16]   See Henry J. Steiner, Ideals and Counter-Ideals ..., supra note, p. 1542.

some kind of personal autonomy by guaranteeing the right to effective participation of persons belonging to national minorities in public affairs affecting them.

What does the term "cultural autonomy" mean? There are several entities which have been granted "autonomy" not as a response to desires for political self-government, but rather as a means of guaranteeing ethnic or linguistic groups a degree of independence from governmental interference in matters of particular concern to these groups, e.g., cultural autonomy [17]. The effect of the relevant statutory or other provisions in these cases is to protect certain cultural peculiarities, customs, practices, and societal structures from interference on the part of the central or sovereign government. The FUEN draft convention (art.7) defines cultural autonomy as a right of ethnic groups "not forming the majority of population" to established associations with public law status which will be "administered by bodies elected freely according to democratic principles". According to FUEN, the cultural autonomy consists in autonomous managing of culture, education, information etc. and in establishing and maintaining institutions in these fields by autonomous decisions (art.8) [18]. The term culture should be defined in a broad sense. It should cover not only art and literature but also a way of thinking, tradition, moral principles, the way of life of living etc. [19] Culture can not exist without freedom in general, which provide the human spirit with the necessary creativity, or without the freedom of thought. The right to culture is a collective right. Capotorti stated in his UN-sponsored study that the sense of the obligations of states is to maintain and develop the cultural identity of minorities, and that the states are obliged to adopt the necessary measures for reaching these goals [20]. Granting cultural autonomy is one of the possible responses of governments to the needs of minorities in this field. But the degree of cultural independence enjoyed by minorities in this model does not include sufficient political or legal control over internal matters to constitute full autonomy [21].

---

[17]   Hannum, Hurst/lillich, Richard B., The concept of Autonomy in International Law, in Dinstein, Yoram (Ed.), Models of Autonomy (New Brunswick, London, 1981), p. 246.

[18]   FUEN Draft Convention, supra note, p. 58-59.

[19]   Devetak, Silvo, Manjine, ljudska prava, demokratija (Minorities, Human rights, Democracy), (Oslobodjenje, Sarajevo, 1988), p. 256.

[20]   See Capotorti, Study on the Rights of Persons belonging to the Ethnic, Religious and Kinguistic Minorities, New York, United Nations, 1979, p.100, para. 599.

[21]   Hannum/Lillich listed the following elements of full autonomy: locally - elected body with some independent legislative power; locally-chosen chief executive; independent local judiciary; power-sharing between the central and autonomous government. Ibid, p.252.

After the collapse of the three European federations the notion of territorial minority autonomy is scarcely to be found in the legal and political systems of the European states but the outstanding cases of South Tyrol / Alto Adige and Aaland Islands. On the contrary, the expulsion and annihilation of ethnic and religious minorities has become an integral part of the European political reality. The inter-ethnic annihilation what will become known world-wide as ethnic cleansing wasn't a by-product of the armed conflict on the territory of former Yugoslavia, but the main goal of the warfare for new borders and for the "ethnically purified" demographic composition of the new Nation-states [22]. The legislation on citizenship has been another tool for "soft" ethnic cleansing of the democratic structure of the new European Nation-states, along with social consequences of the economic crisis which as a rule hit first of all the members of "other ethnicity" and force many of them to leave the territories where they used to live and work [23].

New demands and arguments

The quest for autonomy has become nonetheless one of the basic claims of many minority movements. Policies of the majority or dominant groups in a society may lessen tensions or, by denying minority groups fair shares or opportunities, may exacerbate problems to the point of risking conflict that threatens social order. In these latter circumstances, the claims of ethnic minorities for autonomy schemes will become most insistent [24].

The Federal Republic of Yugoslavia

The legal protection of ethnic minorities in the FRY should be considered in the whole complex of the political crisis that had begun with the nationalistic Albanian rebellion in Kosovo in 1982, continued with the brutal repression against the Albanians, with the raise of the Serbian nationalism and the abolition of the autonomous status of Kosovo and Vojvodina in 1989, and culminated with the establishment of the parallel Albanian authorities in Kosovo (and abroad), with inter-ethnic tensions and the influx of more then 300 000 refuges of Serb origin from Croatia and Bosnia who change the demographic composition of the population and opened new political and socio-economic problems In the framework of the constitutional order of the FRY the new "autonomous provinces" of Kosovo

---

[22] As the result, has after 1991 dramatically changed especially the ethnic structure of the population of parts of Bosnia and Hercegovina under the control of the Serbs (Republika Srbska) and Croats (Herceg-Bosna), as well as of Croatia, after the expulsion or emigration of a great majority of the Serb population (its share in the total population decreased from 12,2% in 1991 to estimated 2-3% in 1995). As illustration of many sources available see Situation of Human rights in the Territory of the former Yugoslavia, Periodic report, Ethnic Cleansing of Eastern Enclaves, ECOSOC, E/CN.4/1994/3 of 5 May 1993 and Second periodic report, Ethnic Cleansing by Croat Forces, ECOSOC, E/CN.4/1994/4 of 19 May 1993,

[23] The law of Croatia on citizenship of 1991, for instance, requires that citizenship depends, among other things, on a conclusion that an applicant is "attached to the legal system and customs persisting in the Republic of Croatia and that he or she accepts the Croatian culture" (art.8). According to art.26 of the same law, the Ministry of Interior may deny a petition for citizenship "if it is the opinion that there are reasons of interest for the Republic of Croatia" for such a denial. See also Situation of human rights in the territory of the former Yugoslavia. ECOSOC, Commision on Human Rights, E/CN.4//1997/8 of 25 October 1996, pp.30-31.

[24] SeeHenry J. Steiner, supra note, p. 1542.

and Metohija and Vojvodina are no more the legal framework for the regulation of minorities issues [25]. In 1993 were, also formally, abolished all the laws adopted by the two provinces [26]. Article 109 of the Constitution of Serbia assigned to "autonomous provinces" the competencies to "adopt general enactment in the fields of culture, education, and official use of language". But the Parliament of Serbia must give in advance the consent for the adoption of the Statute of the "autonomous province". Nevertheless the "autonomous province" have formally the assembly, the executive council and the administration [27].

The constitutional structure of the FRY ensures to national minorities [28]. A great number of "specific" rights [29], mostly concerning the use of language, education and culture. The constitutions include some elements of ethnic autonomy: the right of minorities to establish cultural institutions and associations (art.47 of the constitution of the FRY), the obligation of the republic to ensure the equal representation of minorities in public services and in state and local government (chapter 5 and art.73 of the constitutions of Serbia and Montenegro respectively), the right to take part in the regional and international organisations and the right to address the international organisations in order to protect their freedoms and rights guaranteed by the constitution (art.74/2 of the Montenegro constitution); the participation of minorities in the Council for the protection of the rights of national and ethnic groups, which is chaired by the President of the Republic of Montenegro which supervise the preparation of legislation and formulation of government policies in the field of minority protection (art.76 of the constitution of Montenegro) [30]. Unfortunately, there are not relevant analysis and surveys on the implementation of the constitutional rights of minorities in FRY.

In the "autonomous province" of Vojvodina two political organisations, the Democratic Community of the Hungarians of Vojvodina (DZVM) and the Alliance of the Hungarians of Vojvodina (SVM) dominate among the members of Hungarian minority, after the split in 1994. In the elections for the Chamber of citizens of the Federal Parliament held on 3 November 1996, the SVM elected three representatives and the DZVM none.

The DZVM program for autonomies has had three stages: 1) personal and cultural autonomy regardless of the territory, 2) local self-government in settlements in which a minority constitutes a majority, and 3) the establishment of the Hungarian autonomous area/region with the seat in Subotica/Szabadka which should include seven "territorially contiguous administrative units/districts of

[25] Official Gazette of the RS n° 1/1990; Official Gazette of Montenegro n° 48/1992; Official Gazette of the FR of Yugoslavia, n° 1 of 27 april 1992.

[26] Official Gazette of the FRY n° 20 of 11 november 1993.

[27] BalÜa èpadijer, PolitiΦki sistem Jugoslavije i manjinsko pitanje (The Political System of Yugoslavia and the minority issue), Konferencija "PoloЯaj manjina u Jugoslaviji", Beograd, 11-13 januar 1995, p.4

[28] In the constitution of FRY is used the term "national minorities", of Serbia "nationalities", and of Montenegro "national or ethnic groups"

[29] Marjana PajvanΦiμ, Ustavno pravo (Constitutional law). Novi Sad: Centar za izdavaΦku delatnost, Univerzitet Novi Sad, 1993, pp.224-25.

[30] On the situation of minorities in FRY see also Situation of human rights in the territory of the former Yugoslavia, Special report on minorities, ECOSOC. E/CN.4/1997/8 of 25 October 1996.

Hungarian majority with the most significant settlements" [31]. The realisation of autonomy has been interpreted by the authors of the notion above as a "restricted sovereignty of the minority" [32].

The SVM to the contrary advocates autonomy for the entire province of Vojvodina, and autonomy for Hungarians within it. The party wants either a sort of territorial autonomy in the Northern Backa region, which includes the seven municipalities with a major portion of Hungarian population, or the establishment of a separate region of Northern Backa. The party sees the way forward for Vojvodina Hungarians in dialogue with Belgrade, that is, with the government and parliamentary parties.

The third minority party in Vojvodina, the Democratic Union of Croats in Vojvodina (DSHV), wants cultural and educational autonomy for Croats in FRY. This would mean freedom for the Croatian community to organise their own institutions and schools, which would be financed by state. It would also mean representation of Croats in the mass media, through special sections and programmes. According to the leaders of DSHV all this would be implemented and supervised by a Croatian National Council, for which there is still no legal basis [33]. The DSHV in recent elections didn't manage to elect a representative to the Federal Parliament.

In Vojvodina, unlike Kosovo, autonomy is not an interethnic issue, but one which divide Serb public opinion and political opposition [34]. The viewpoint of the opposition on autonomy in Vojvodina doesn't differ from that of the ruling party [35]. The Zajedno coalition has made no attempts to gather under its wing the political groups which signed or indirectly supported the autonomist Manifesto for Vojvodina, published at the end of 1995 by a group of independent deputies in the Vojvodina Assembly and other organisations [36]. The Vojvodina Serbs have not organised any large pro-autonomy political party, although the small parties have managed to form a coalition [37] and to elect two representatives in the Federal Parliament.

---

[31] Memorandum on the Self-Government of Hungarians in the Republic of Serbia, Working Document at the General Assembly of the Democratic Community of Hungarians in Vojvodina, April 25, 1992

[32] Pal èandor, Koncept manjinske samouprave Demokratske zajednice Vojvodjanskih MadPiara (The concept of minorities' self-management of The democratic community of the Hungarians of Vojvodina). Beograd: Dec.1994.

[33] Josip Stantic, Minorities Struggle Against Marginalisation, Wareport, 46, oct. 1996, p. 38.

[34] Dragan Veselinov, Autonomy - Who wants it?, War report, London, Febr. 1995.

[35] The general problem related with the efficiency of the Yugoslav political oposition is that they have not develop an alternative political programme in respect of that of Miloshevich, for instance, in regard of Kosovo syndrome, the Vojvodina autonomy, and the relations with their brothers in Bosnia and Herzegovina, some of them being in the latest issue even more linked with nationalistic groups of the regime in Republika Srbska.

[36] Jan Briza, Manifesto for Autonomy, Wareport, 38, Nov./Déc. 1995.

[37] Dimitrije Boarov, The Autonomy Debate, Wareport, 46, Oct.1996, p.37.

The Muslim Party of Democratic Action (SDA, as in Bosnia and Herzegovina), organised in October 1991 an referendum on autonomy for the region of Sandzak. According to SDA 98.9 % of the vote cast were in favour of an autonomous Sandzak. The Muslim National Council of Sandzak adopted on June 6, 1993 a Memorandum on the Special Status for Sandzak. According to the incorporated map this region, bordering with Bosnia and Herzegovina, includes eleven municipalities of Serbia and Montenegro. The function of authority shall be carried out by the "governmental bodies" of Sandzak and by the "governmental bodies" of the townships within it, except in those cases specifically provided for in the Memorandum. The Yugoslav authorities would share the responsibility with those of Sandzak for carrying out the following: environmental conservation, federal highways and other major roads, canals, pipelines, postal, telephone and telegraph services, transmission of the electrical energy.

All other matters would be the jurisdiction of the regional "governmental bodies" which will have no right to enter into international relations except those concerning scientific and technical, cultural and educational, and economic collaboration. A part of the Memorandum is also a list with the rights of the Muslim nation, but the rights of the Serb and Montenegrin population (37 % in the Serbian and 63 % in the Montenegrine part of Sandzak) are even not mentioned [38]. The Muslim National Council of Sandzak boycotted the elections of May and December 1992 but took part in the recent elections. The president of the Council, dr.Sulejman Ugljanin, was as a head of the List for Sandzak elected in the Federal Parliament of the FRY.

It is impossible to explain the Kosovo problem in terms of minorities protection or autonomy. The Kosovo Provincial Assembly, which was suspended on 2 July 1990, declared on 22 September 1991 the Republic of Kosovo a sovereign and independent state. In the referendum held on 26-30 September 1991 a full 99.87 % of those who voted (turnout was 87% due to a boycott by local Serbs) affirmed their desire for Kosovo to be a sovereign and independent state [39]. On 24 May 1992 the Assembly organised the general and Presidential elections. The winner was the Democratic League of Kosova (96 deputies in the 130 member Assembly). In the Presidential elections Ibrahim Rugova won by an overwhelming majority [40].

Most Kosovo Albanians working abroad faithfully pay 3% of their income in taxes to the exile Kosovo's government [41]. Non-co-operation with Serbia's authorities and the institutions they now controlled is the main political orientation of the Albanians. They have developed parallel institutions, for instance, in the fields of education, health care and police [42]. The Memorandum, signed on 1 September 1996 by Miloshevich and Rugova, which provoked a fierce reaction by

---

[38]   See Memorandum on the Establishment of a Special Status for Sanjak (Muslim Council of Sanjak, Novi Pazar, 1993)

[39]   Michael Salla, Kosovo, Non-violence and the Break - up of Yugoslavia, Security Dialogue, vol.26(4), 1995, pp.428-29.

[40]   Ibid., p.429.

[41]   Robert Elsie, The Albanian Media in Kosovo and the Spectre of Ethnic Cleansing, Suedosteuropa, 44, 9-10/1995, p.617.

[42]   Michael Salla, supra note, p. 429-30.

Serbian nationalists in Kosovo, has provided the Albanian pupils and teachers with the opportunity to enter the public schools again. It remains to be seen whether the accord will be implemented. It is estimated today that up to 300,000 pupils and 6000 students are attending primary and secondary schools, and the university in Pristina respectively. Since these institutions are not operating under government authority, diplomas and degrees issued by them are not officially recognised [43]. Surveys have shown that only few Albanians want autonomy. The main aim of the majority gathered around the Democratic League of Kosovo is unity with Albania, and they see their declaration of the independence of Kosovo of 1991 (or the proposed international protectorate), simply as transitional stages to that [44].

The Republic of Croatia

The Croatian Constitution, adopted in 1990 [45], proclaims the realisation of "the thousand year old national identity" of the Croatian nation. The document proclaims Croatia to be "the nation state of the Croatian nation and a state of members of other nations and minorities who are its citizens: Serbs, Moslems, Slovenes, Czechs, Slovaks, Italians, Hungarians, Jews and others" [46]. Howard is of the opinion that any citizen who is not ethically Croatian should find the constitution's basic premise unsettling. Defining the state in national or ethnic terms creates an atmosphere of "insiders" and "outsiders" - a distinction between those who are permitted, as a matter of sufferance, to leave in the country [47].

The constitution (art.15) guarantees to "all members of nations and minorities the freedom of expression of their national affiliation, the free use of their own language and script, and the cultural autonomy". The official language of the state is the Croatian language and Latin script (art.12/1). In particular local units it is possible, under the conditions prescribed by law, introduce in the official use, beside the Croatian language and the Latin script, also another language and the Chirilic or another script (art.12/2).

In the context of declaring its independence, in June 1991, has the Parliament of Croatia passed the Charter on the rights of the Serbs and other nationalities in the Republic of Croatia. According to this (political) declaration are all the nationalities in Croatia protected against any activity which could jeopardise their existence, and have the right to be respected, the right to self-protection and to cultural autonomy (point IV). The Serbs and all other nationalities have the right to co-operate, on proportional basis, in the organs of local self-management and in adequate bodies of the state

---

[43]   Situation of human rights on the territory of FRY, supra note, p.13.

[44]   Dragan Veselinov, Autonomy -Who wants it?, War report, London, Febr.1995.

[45]   Narodne novine (Official Gazette of the Republic of Croatia), n° 56 of 22 December 1990.

[46]   According to the census of population of 1981 these ethnic groups represent the following share in the total population of Croatia: Croats: 3.454.661 or 75,07 %; Serbs: 531.502 or 11,55 %; Muslims: 23.740 or 0,52 %; Slovenes: 25.136 or 0,55 %; Hungarians: 25.439 or 0,55 %; Italians: 11.661 or 0,25 %; Slovaks: 6.533 or 0,14 %; Czechs: 15.061 or 0,33 %; Jews: 0,007 %.

[47]   A.E.Dick Howard, Constitutions and Constitutionalism in Central and Eastern Europe, Human Dimension Seminar on the Rule of Law, Selected materials. OSCE, Warsaw, 28 November-1 December 1995, p.7.

authorities; the charter also assured their economic and social development aimed at the protection of their identity and of avoiding any assimilation [48].

The new constitution leaves the elaboration of the future contents of the legal order on the rights of minorities to laws and other enactment (which have not yet been adopted). The new law on the primary schools, for instance, contains only a general provision on the education of children of the "members of nationalities" (art.7) [49]. In this situation it is not clear which "old" laws and other enactment are still valid and, if they are, to which extent. This applies especially to the use of minorities languages, to the upbringing and education in the minorities languages, to the legal status of minorities' societies and organisations, and to the competencies of local self-management units.

The new legal system has left few if any competencies concerning minorities and inter-ethnic relations to new communes and municipalities. As to the competencies of the new districts (Rupanije) which are a part of the state structure suffices to mention the events concerning the statute of the "ethnically mixed" (Croatian-Italian) district of Istria. In February 1995, the Constitutional Court repealed 18 of 36 provisions of the statute, some of them regulating ethnic and linguistic equality, as well as the reference to the international instruments on local self-management [50]. Some leaders of the leading regional party - Istrian Democratic Diet (IDD) are of the opinion that is the first political goal to turn Istria, which is divided between Croatia, Slovenia and Italy, into an autonomous Euroregion [51].

The Parliament of Croatia has established the Committee on human rights. It is composed by the representatives of the Parliamentarian parties and at least one member of minorities [52]. The Committee has nominated the sub-commissions with consultative status "for Croats living abroad" and "for national or ethnic communities or minorities". The government also established in 1990, as its advisory administrative unit, "the office for national minorities" [53]. Later it became "the office for inter-ethnic relations" and in 1995 "the office for ethnic and national communities or minorities" [54]. These changes in the name were the reflection of the military-political events and, as a consequence, of the changing of the ethnic composition of the population of Croatia after 1991.

The "Serbian issue" in Croatia has to be seen in the context of wars between Serbia and Croatia for the division of former Yugoslavia and especially Bosnia and Herzegovina. In illustration of this it suffices to refer to the "Declaration on the inalienable right of the Serb nation to self-determination", adopted by the Parliament of Serbia on 27 December 1991. The Parliament

---

[48]   The text of the Charter: see Official Gazette n° 31 of 25 June 1991.

[49]   Official Gazette n° 59 of 31 December 1990, p.1372.

[50]   Official Gazette n° 9 of 10 February 1995, p. 299.

[51]   Loredana Bogliun Debeljuh, The Istrian Euroregion. Socio-Cultural Situation and Problems. In: The Yugoslav War, Europe and the Balkans: How to Achieve Security?, eds.S.Bianchini and P.Shoup. Ravenna: Longo Editore, 1995, p.95.

[52]   Official Gazettes n° 53 of 14 December 1990, p.1137 and n° 59 of 29 September 1992, p.1317.

[53]   Official Gazette n° 52 of 12 Décember 1990.

[54]   Official Gazette n° 62 of 1 September 1995, p. 1776.

recognised the legality of the decision of the Serb nation living outside Serbia to "live... in Yugoslavia" [55]. Under the pressure of the international community has Croatia on 4 December 1991 adopted the "Constitutional law on human rights and liberties and on the rights of ethnic and national communities and minorities in the Republic of Croatia". The law was in fact one of the conditions for its international recognition. The final text, obviously after being amended, was "acknowledged" by the legal committee of the Parliament on 3 June 1992 [56].

The law has 65 articles. A great majority of them deal with the rights of the Serbian minority [57]. The most important were three provisions: a. the right of cultural autonomy (art.6), b. the right of the Serbs (which had at the adoption of the law constituted more than 8 % of the total population of Croatia), to be proportionally represented in the Parliament, government and supreme judicial bodies, and of others minorities to have altogether 5 representatives in the Parliament" (art.18), and c. the right to establish two "counties with special self-managing - autonomous - status" (Knin and Glina) which will include 11 communes where the Serbs constitute, according the census of 1981, the majority population (art.22). Articles 21 to 61 prescribe in details the organisation and competencies of these autonomies. According to this law the Serbs had the constitutional right to be represented by at least 12,2 % or by 13 members of the Parliament, and by the same percentage in government and judiciary as well [58].

The number of Serbian population in Croatia (without Eastern Slavonia) has been dramatically reduced, from 12,2 % in 1991 to the estimated 2-3 % of the total population in 1995. As result of the military actions against the "Serb rebellion" in Krajina, in May and August 1995, have about 150-200.00 of the remaining Croatian Serbs fled the country and settled as refuges, either in Bosnia and the FR of Yugoslavia or in Eastern Slavonia (which is now in the process of "peaceful re-integration" with Croatia). In order to "legitimate" the new demographic situation, the Parliament on 20 September 1995 suspended several basic articles of the Constitutional law on human rights and minorities of 1991. The suspension included all the above mentioned rights of the Serbian minority, explicitly those concerning their proportional representation and the ethnic autonomy [59].

In addition, new provisions were adopted (the amendments of the law on elections - art.58a/3, 4, 5, 6, [60], the law on the electorate districts, the "obligatory directives" of the president of the state commission for elections) prescribing that will on special "minority lists" the Serbs elect 3, and other

[55]   Official Gazette of the Republic of Serbia n° 79 of 31 December 1991, pp.3360-61.

[56]   Official Gazette n° 34 of June 1992.

[57]   Smiljko Sokol and Branko Smerdel, Ustavno pravo (Constitutional Law). Informator, Zagreb, 1995, p.71-72.

[58]   These representatives will be elected as other representatives, on the parties'list; if in this way the required number will not be obtained, will be enlarged the number of elected representatives in order to get the required number; if also this will be not successful, will the President of the Republic declare new elections for the number of Serb representatives that fail. See, Sokol and Smerdel, Ustavno pravo (Constitutional Law). Informator, Zagreb: 1995, p.164.

[59]   The text of this law see in Official Gazette n° 68 of 21 October 1995, p.1833.

[60]   Official Gazette n° 68 of 21 September 1995, p. 1836.

minorities 4 representatives [61]. The Croats living abroad, mostly in Bosnia and Herzegovina, elect 12 representatives to the Parliament of the Republic of Croatia [62]. These provisions contravene art.18 of the amended "constitutional law" on the rights of minorities which prescribes the election of 5 representatives of "other minorities"[63]. As to the Serbs, it is not clear on which basis has the legislator decided to "give them" 3 mandates, thus replacing their suspended constitutional right to "proportional representation" with 13 mandates. On the last elections in Croatia (November 1995) were on the minorities' lists elected 4 MP representing the Czech and Slovak, the Hungarian, Ruthenian, Ukrainian, German and Austrian, and Italian minorities [64].

The adoption of laws providing a legal basis for the settlement (by ethnic Croats) of territories left by Serbs was a final stroke to the constitutional law on the ethnic autonomy for the Serbian population in Croatia. On 20 September 1995, one month after the military action in Krajina, the new law prescribes the "temporarily possession and administration" by the government of all property of the Serbs who have left the country after the beginning of armed conflict in 1990 and live in the FR of Yugoslavia or in "the occupied territories of Bosnia and Herzegovina"(probably in the territories under Serbian control). The same will happened with the property of the citizens of the FR of Yugoslavia in Croatia.

The government has the right (art.5) to give this real property "in temporary possession and use" to the displaced persons and refuges, to the Croatian emigrants who have returned to the country and whose property was damaged or lost in the war, to the families whose members have died or disappeared in war, and "to all other citizens who are fulfilling activities which are necessary for the security, reconstruction and development" of these territories [65]. The same applies also to the "members of the Croatian nation who came as refuges from the parts of Bosnia and Herzegovina under Serb occupation, and from Serbia or Montenegro" [66].

On the same day was adopted the law which gives to the government of Croatia the right to rent the apartments of the Serbs (who fled and will not return in "90 days after entering of the law in force") to persons whose activities are of public interests and accept the obligation to remain in these places at least 3 years [67]. Moreover, the small number of the Serbian population that remains on this territory live in a state of insecurity. The Special Rapporteur of the OUN Commission on Human Rights had on 22 August 1996 stated "that there apparently is an unwillingness on the part of the Croatian authorities to take strong preventive measures to ensure the safety of local residents". She was "deeply

---

[61]   Official Gazette n° 82 of 12 October 1995, p. 2295.

[62]   The text of the law see in the Official Gazette n° 68 of 21 September 1995, art. 3 and 5, p. 1836.

[63]   Official Gazette n° 68 of 21 October 1995, art. 2 and 3, p. 1833.

[64]   M. Domini and B.Vukas (1995), Prava i slobode etniФkih i nacionalnih zajednica/manjina. In: Demokratske slobode u Hrvatskoj. Zagreb: Europski pokret Hrvatske, p.30.

[65]   Official Gazette n° 73 of 27 September 1995, p. 1919.

[66]   Art. 11 of the Regulation on the return of displaced persons and refugees to the liberated territories, Official Gazette n° 81 of 10 October 1995.

[67]   Official Gazette n° 73 of 27 September 1995, p. 1921.

concerned at this situation for many reasons, including its likely effect on the decisions of Croatian Serbs who are considering either remaining in - or returning to - the area..."[68].

Former Yugoslav Republic of Macedonia

The most sensitive issue for the new Macedonian state are relations with the Albanian population. The majority of the republic population in 1994 were ethnic Macedonians (1,288,330 or 66,52%); they traditionally belonged to the Macedonian Orthodox Church. The second largest ethnic group were that of the Albanians who officially are said to number 442,914 or 22.87%; Albanian leaders contest this figure and suggest that closer to 40% of the population is Albanian [69].

Article 38 of the Constitution of FYROM guarantees the protection of identity of the nationalities (ethnic minorities) [70]. It prescribes the right 1) to freely express, foster and develop their identity, 2) to establish institutions for culture and art, as well as scholarly and other associations for the expression, fostering and development of their identity, 3) to instruction in their language in primary and secondary education, as determined by law (in these schools is the Macedonian language a mandatory subject).

The Macedonian language (written in Cyrillic alphabet) is the official language of the republic (art.7/1). The languages and alphabets of the nationalities would be, according the constitution, in official use, in addition to Macedonian (in manner determined by law that was not yet adopted), "in the units of self-government where they constitute the majority of population" (art.7/2) as well as in the units where they live "in considerable number" (art.7/3).

The Parliament establishes a Council for Inter-Ethnic Relations (art.78). Its competence is to "consider issues of inter-ethnic relations in the Republic and to make appraisals and proposals for their solution" which must be taken into consideration by the Parliament when it is making decisions regarding these matters. Ethnic minorities had elected in 1994 altogether 22 members of 120 members of the Parliament (Albanians - 19, Turks - 1, Roma - 1, Serbs - 1). The current coalition cabinet, includes five Albanian ministers out of 22 cabinet posts. Of political significance is also the increased number of Albanian recruits in the army. Whereas in 1992, only 7.5% of the Army of the Republic of Macedonia recruits were Albanian, in 1993 fully 26.5% were Albanian [71].

The Albanians feel separate and unequal in the Macedonian state and are seeking to have equal constituent status with the majority Macedonians [72]. They object to the designation of Macedonian, with its Cyrillic alphabet, as the only official language of the state. To combat this, they demand, among other things, the establishment of Albanian language secondary schools and the university, and the official use of the Albanian flag, symbol not only of the Albanian state, but of the nation. In 1995 the

---

[68] See Situation of human rights in the territory of the former Yugoslavia, Special report on minorities. ECOSOC, E/CN.4/1997/8 of 25 October 1996, p.32.

[69] Duncan M.Perry, Crisis in the making? Macedonia and its Neighbors, Suedost Europa, 43, no.1-2/1994, p.35.

[70] The texte of the Constitution see in Official Gazette n° 52 of 22 November 1991.

[71] Duncan M. Perry, supra note, p. 38.

[72] Ibid, p. 35.

Parliament didn't accept the Albanians' request for bilingual ID what was the cause for resignation of one of the leading Albanian politician from the post of the Vice-chairman of the Parliament.

Albanians claim that article 45 of the constitution referring to the establishing of private schools "at all levels of education" provide them with the legal basis for the establishment of the private Albanian university in Tetovo where they constitute a great majority of 130.000 out of the total of 181.000 inhabitants. To the opposite, the government is of the opinion that only the Parliament can pass such decisions and that there is not need for the university as the Albanians have such facilities at the universities of Skopje and Bitola (in the later city the Albanians constitute a tiny minority with 4800 out of the total of 125.000 inhabitants).

Should the Albanians not achieve their goals, anything from intensive legal action to an autonomy declaration to secession is threatened [73]. Already in 1992, a small group of Albanian nationalists declared the creation of the autonomous Ilirida Republic in the Struga area, although it has had tittle impact at the time. In the January 1992 the Albanians organised a referendum on their status which was declared illegal by the government. 74 % out of 92% of those eligible to vote who participated in a referendum voted for the autonomy for Albanians. The idea of unification of all the seven million or so Albanians living in the Balkans is more and more present also among the Macedonian Albanians.

The Republic of Slovenia

The status and rights of the Hungarian and Italian "national communities" represent a mixture of elements of territorial, functional ("take part clause", representation), personal and cultural autonomy, while would the Roma (Gypsies) enjoy (art. 65 of the constitution) a limited cultural autonomy, concerning mainly primary education, what should be determined by the statute (that was not yet adopted). The rights of minorities should be implemented regardless their numerical strength (art. 64, par. 4 of the constitution). This obviously applies first of all to the implementation of the elements of different intermingled kinds of autonomy, exercised by the members of the Italian and Hungarian minorities.

The legal system of Slovenia is based on the notion of "ethnically mixed territories" that were before 30 years established by a list of "ethnically mixed locations" enshrined in the statutes of the communes Murska Sobota and Lendava/Lendva (Hungarians) and Koper/Capodistria, Izola/Isola, and Piran/Pirano (Italians). With the reform of the local self-government 157 municipalities have been founded in 1994, replacing 61 former communes, including the five with "ethnically mixed territories". By the new law on the establishment of municipalities and the determination of their territory [74], a part of the ethnically mixed area populated with Hungarians has been placed into other municipalities than they were before, whilst all ethnically mixed areas along the border with Italy where the Italian minority live remained in the same municipalities as they were before the change of legislation [75].

---

[73]   Ibid, p. 36.

[74]   Official Gazette of the Republic of Slovenia, n° 60/94 adopted on 3 October 1994.

[75]   In illustration see art.7 of the Statute of the municipality of Koper/Capodistria, Primorske novice, Official announcements, No.9/95 of 25 May 1995.

Participation in decision making. The laws on the elections of deputies in the State chamber of 1992 [76] and in the councils of new municipalities from 1993 [77] prescribe that both "national communities" are mandatory represented by one deputy each in the State Chamber, and (together with Roma) by at least one member of the councils of the new ethnically mixed six municipalities. The law on self-government (art. 72) [78] provides the "ethnically mixed" (and other interested) municipalities with the option of establishing a region in order to "resolve the issues concerning the realisation of the rights and statutory provisions prescribed by the constitution". This choice is not of significant interest either to "majority" or to "minority" due to the very meagre competencies of the units which could be join in the region. In addition, this law (art. 39) prescribes the right of minorities representatives to veto the municipalities enactment concerning the financing of their needs. In the ethnically mixed municipalities commissions for ethnic questions will be established, of which one half will be composed by minorities and the other by majority members. According to the law on self-managing national communities of 1994 [79] are the bodies of the local self-government communities obliged to deal with proposals, initiatives and opinions given by self-managing national communities (art.12). The State Chamber, the government and other state agencies (art.15) are requested to ask for the opinion of the national communities whenever decide on the matters related to their status.

Personal autonomy. The above mentioned law prescribes special rights of Italian and Hungarian minorities regarding their organising on the territories where they live, concerning relationships between their organisations and state agencies or local bodies as well as their international co-operation. According to article 3 is the "self-managing national community" a public legal person performing following tasks: 1) deciding autonomously on all matters within its competence in accordance with the constitution and law; 2) giving consent, in accordance with law, to matters concerning the protection of special rights of national communities; 3) discussing and studying matters concerning its status, and adopting opinions and submitting proposals and initiatives to competent bodies; 4) stimulating and organising activities contributing to the preservation of ethnic identity of members of the two national communities. Minorities' representatives in the State Chamber and municipalities councils as well as the members of the bodies of the minorities self-management communities, are elected by minorities voters - wherever in the state they live - who are on the "electoral list" prepared by both ethnic self-governing organisations. The principle of personal autonomy is expressed also by the right of the members of Hungarian and Italian minorities to learn their languages, on facultative basis, in secondary schools outside the ethnically mixed territories if at least 6-7 pupils express this wish (until now one case).

Cultural autonomy. Elements of cultural autonomy could be seen especially in the organisation of education. On the basis of the law on the organisation and financing of education [80] and the law on institutes[81] (both of 1991) are the ethnic communities the co-founders of primary and secondary schools and are mandatory represented in the school councils. Both "national communities" autonomously run the publishing of newspapers, periodicals and books in their respective languages.

---

[76]   Official Gazette of the Republic of Slovenia, n° 44/92.

[77]   Official Gazette of the Republic of Slovenia n° 72/93.

[78]   Official Gazette of the Republic of Slovenia, n° 72/93 and 57/94.

[79]   Official Gazette of the Republic of Slovenia, n° 65/94 of 20 October 1994.

[80]   Official Gazette of the Republic of Slovenia, n° 12/91.

[81]   Ibidem.

The public libraries on ethnically mixed territories - in the councils of which are the ethnic communities duly represented, on the basis of the respective law - have separate units with literature in the minorities languages.

In accordance with the law on institutes has the Hungarian national community established the institutes for culture and for information. This action is in accordance with art.40 of the law on mass media [82]. The Italian minority has no institutes of this kind but exercise "autonomous influence" on managing its local TV and broadcasting studio (which is formally a part of national/state programme), through the programme council, and by giving opinions for the nomination of the director of the programme (who is appointed by the Council of RTV) and the editors. Members of the Italian minority are not satisfied with the situation in this regard. Both minorities have the right, according to the law on the broadcasting and TV to nominate one member each of the Council of the RTV (art.16) and two third of the members [83] of the council for minorities' programmes (art.22). The law has stipulated that until 1 January 1996 a "minimal Hungarian national programme" should be established (art.30) what wasn't yet realised.

Requests for abolition of minorities rights. The constitutional rights of the Hungarian and Italian minorities were several times challenged by the requests of citizens of the Slovenian majority that the Constitutional court of Slovenia declared as un-constitutional different rights provided by the constitutions of 1974 and 1991 respectively. In 1979 and 1987 respectively the court didn't accepted the requests to declare the bilingual ID and the municipal decision on the national flag of the Hungarian minority as un-constitutional enactment. On July 14, 1995 has the group "Slovenian Istria", represented by seven citizens, begun a constitutional procedure requesting that the court declare as an un-constitutional enactment the provisions of some laws regulating the rights of minorities in Slovenia, i.e., the laws on the evidence of the electoral right, on the elections to the State Chamber, on the self-managed ethnic communities, on the local elections, as well as of the Statute of the municipality of Koper/Capodistria. The Constitutional court of Slovenia has not yet made a decision on this proposal. Its eventual acceptance would essentially change the legal status and the rights of the Hungarian and Italian ethnic communities in Slovenia.

The Cases of Romania and Slovakia

The Hungarian minorities in Romania and Slovakia represent a special case because of their numerical strength [84] and because of the impact of this issue on security in the region and especially on the relations of these two states with Hungary. In 1992 the Hungarian Government made explicit its position on the status it consider desirable for minorities: territorial autonomy when the minorities

---

[82]   Official Gazette of the Republic of Slovenia, n° 18/94, adopted on April 1994.

[83]   Official Gazette of the Republic of Slovenia, n° 18/94, adopted on 8 April 1994.

[84]   The Hungarian population numbers 1,6 million (7,1 % of the population) but their absolute number is falling (there were 1,7 million in 1977, or 7,9% of the population). In Slovakia the Hungarian minority represents about 600,000 people or 12% of the population.

are in the majority at local level; administrative and cultural autonomy in the other cases [85]. Many Hungarian authors supported these claims [86].

As to Romania the congress of the DUHR - the Democratic Union of Hungarians in Romania - which was held in January 1993 declared its acceptance of the frontiers and relinquished its demand for territorial autonomy. On the other hand, the aim of cultural autonomy and of a degree of freedom in local government has been retained.[87] The requests for different kinds of autonomy of Hungarians in Romania are motivated also by the fact that they represent the majority population of two administrative regions in Transylvania, Hargita and Covasna (84,5% and 75,2% respectively) as well as 23,9% of population of Transylvania, 21,2% of Crisana - Marumures and 6,6% of Banat [88].

In the documents adopted by the 4th congress of DUHR held in Cluj/Kolosvar in 1995 the autonomy was defined as "a right exercised by the national community aiming to defend, express, develop and preserve its national identity" and "a means for the Hungarian community to found its economic and cultural development in its motherland" [89]. The autonomy based on personal principle provides the Hungarians, according to DUHR, with the framework to establish an own system of educational, cultural and informative institutions, and for preserving traditions and protecting monuments. The territorial autonomy should be applied in administrative units "where the proportion of the persons belonging to national minorities is considerable". Such autonomy should be approved by population through referendum and exercised by local self-governments with special status [90].

In the framework of this political concept concerning autonomy the DUHR requested among other a) the establishment of an autonomous network of cultural institutions and of a native - language educational network, which comprises "all levels and forms of instruction and training", b) the guaranteeing of the functioning of independent Hungarian TV and radio stations, c) the proportional share of the funds allocated for cultural and educational purposes in the state budget [91], d) the modification of those laws and regulations, which are inconsistent with the principle of autonomy of local self-governments or comprise discriminatory provisions in respect of national minorities (especially the aboloshment of law no.69/1991, and the amendment of the law 18/1990 and of several

---

[85]   Michel Foucher, supra note, p. 45.

[86]   Lajos Arday is of the opinion that "granting personal, cultural self-determination and territorial autonomy should be considered as the most important way of putting minority rights into practice". See L.A., Majority versus Minority: Autonomous Schemes and Security Risks in Central and Southeastern Europe (1995), In: Minderheiten als Konfliktpotential in Ostmittel - und Suedosteuropa. Muenchen: R.Oldenbourg Verlag, pp. 54-69.

[87]   Michel Foucher, supra note, p. 46.

[88]   Michel Foucher, supra note, p. 37.

[89]   Democratic Alliance of Hungarians in Romania, Documents (1995), Cluj, p. 6.

[90]   Ibid, p. 6.

[91]   Ibid, p. 7.

provisions concerning language use, education, health care etc.) [92], and the establishment of new micro regions and attraction areas [93].

The Hungarian minority has established a great number of it own organisations and foundations for supporting education, science, cultural life, publications of books and magazines etc. Due to the lack of funds in Romania is a great deal of this activity gaining support from beyond the boundary, i.e. from Hungary. The DUHR has withdrawn from the Council of National Minorities in Bucharest because "the government hasn't observed any of the political decisions which were taken by the Council to arrange the situation of minorities" and is of the opinion that the Council "serves only for political window dressing" [94].

The Romanian legislation fell short concerning the requests of the Hungarian minority for ethnic autonomy. The Law on Local Public Administration (No.69/1991) doesn't even mention ethnic autonomy and contains only three provisions regarding the use of minority's mother tongue in relations with the territorial administrative units. The Law on the Elections for the House of Deputies and the Senate (No.68/1992) provides in art.4, para 1 that "the legally created organisations of citizens belonging to national minority, which have not obtained at least one seat of deputy or senator are entitled...to a seat of deputy if their total number of votes is equal to at least 5% of the average number of valid votes at all country level needed for the election of deputy." The Law on Education of 28 June 1995 doesn't provide minorities with any possibility for taking part in managing the educational institutions or in the creating of programmes regarding minorities.

The "take part clause" concerning the participation of minorities (through their elected representatives in bodies of central or local public authorities), in resolving issues of national or local interest, and the obligation of the authorities to consult them, in accordance with the law, are included in art.15, para.5 of the Hungaro - Romanian treaty on good neighbourhood of September 1996. In appendix to this agreement both parties agreed that the mentioning of the Recommendation 1201 of the Parliamentary Assembly of the Council of Europe does not obligate them to grant the members of minorities "a special territorial autonomy status based on ethnic criteria".

The representatives of the Hungarian minority in Slovakia presented to the Parliament on October 9, 1993 the following demands: 1) cultural and educational autonomy, 2) a new law on names and surnames (tolerating the Hungarian version and transcription to Hungarians), 3) the legal use of bilingual inscriptions and of Hungarian language as a official language in the ethnically mixed territory, and 4) decentralisation of the competencies in accordance with self-government at the national and regional levels [95].

---

[92]   Ibid, p. 20.

[93]   Ibid, p. 21.

[94]   Democratic Alliance of Hungarians in Romania, The Self-organisation of the Intellectual Life of the Hungarians from Romania 1990-1996, Cultural and Cultic Department (1996), Paper distributed at the FUEN Congress in Temisvar, p.4

[95]   Miroslav Kusy, Minority Rights and Nationality Problems in Slovakia, Paper presented at the University of Essex, UK, June 1994, p.5.

This minority is geographically situated on the frontier, a factor which is a specific element in the relations between Slovakia and Hungary. The two countries finally signed on March 19, 1995 a treaty on "good neighbourly relations and friendly co-operation" [96]. Art.15 paragraph 4 (b) refers to the draft Protocol included in the Recommendation 1201 (1993), but the Government of Slovakia, when ratifying it declares that "at no time did it accept or enshrine in the treaty any formulation founded on recognition of the principle of collective rights for minorities or allowing of the creation of autonomous structures on an ethnic basis" [97]. Some authors are of the opinion that militant separationist movements will try to undermine democracy if the Slovak politicians will not manage the improvement of the socio-economic situation and that the deterioration of the position of minorities will intensify the political tensions between Hungary and Slovakia [98].

Former USSR

The eventual outburst of larger ethnic confrontations in Russian federation or the accelerated growth of Russian nationalism would have a disastrous consequences for the stability of the successor states and for European security as a whole. The notion of ethnic autonomy could be one of the tools for accommodating the requirements of ethnic movements and for taking impetus to the nationalistic favour. The cases of Crimean peninsula, Transnistria and the cultural autonomy in Baltic states have in common that all of them are related with the status of the Russian population in the newly established Nation-states after the collapse of the Soviet Union.

According to the census of population of 1989 25.3 million of ethnic Russians lived outside Russia. Besides, more than 10 millions persons chose Russian as their native language. Thus more than 35 million of Russians and Russian-speaking people have lived in 14 independent states of former USSR [99]. This figure have after the dissolution of USSR changed but nevertheless the situation and political orientation of the Russian population in the successor states remains a Pandora box of the European security and stability.

The Russian Federation

Administratively today's Russia consists of eighty seven units. There are twenty-one republics, ten autonomous districts and one autonomous region. One source of possible future conflicts is the national and territorial disbalance. For example, the largest ethnic group - the Russians - are 81.5% of the population, but 51.3% of Russia's territory belong to the national territorial structures, where the

---

[96]   The text see in : Current Policy (1995/5), Ministry of Foreign Affairs, Republic of Hungary, Budapest.

[97]   Council of Europe, Venice Commission, Opinion on the interpretation of article 11 of the draft Protocol to the European Convention on Human Rights appended to the Recommendation 1201 of the Parliamentary Assembly, CDL-INF (96)4 of 22 March 1996, p.4.

[98]   Theo van den Doel, Central Europe: the New Allies? (1994). Boulder-San Francisco-Oxford: Westview Press, pp.35-36.

[99]   Nikolai P.Kolikov, The New Russian Minorities, Report to the Symposium "Ethnies, Minderheiten, Regionen - Baustein oder Sprengstoff Europas, Brno, 27-30 October 1994.

original population are often a slight minority [100]. These territories are frequently rich with natural resources. Almost all Russia's oil is being produced on territories that belong to one autonomous district (Khanty-Mansiysk), and three republics (Tartarstan, Bashkiria and Komi) [101]. Inter-ethnic relations in the Russian federation are burdened with the remnants of the former political notions concerning the "national question" and with new complications as a part of the unsatisfactory endeavours to find out new ways and means for the political and economic stabilisation of the country. On 22 May 1996 has the State Duma adopted a federal law on national - cultural autonomies [102]. The law defines the concept of national - cultural autonomies, the basic rules for their establishment, functioning and termination, their legal status and rights (art.1-6), the protection and the use of national (mother) tongues, and the preservation and development of national cultures (art. 8-15) and the principles for financing the system of national - cultural autonomies (art.16 - 20). Consultative councils with the executive organs on the federal level, as well as on the level of federal units and of cities' self-government, will have an important role in the work of autonomies and in the co-ordination and development of their activities as well (art.7).

The Crimean peninsula

The attempts for the legal definition of the autonomous status of Crimea on territorial basis should be seen in the context of Russia - Ukraine relations and especially in the context of distinctive endeavours of a great majority of Russian population (67% of the peninsula and 22% of the total Ukraine's population), backed by strong political circles in Moscow, [103] to change the decision of 1954 on the inclusion of Crimea in the Ukrainian Socialist Republic and to create, step by step the adequate circumstances for secession. These endeavours have been contested mostly by Ukrainian population (25,7% of total) and has been provoking disputes and tensions with the Ukrainian central authorities in Kiev, between pro-Russian separatists and Ukrainian radical nationalists and between Ukraine and Russia as well.

The legal and constitutional disputes with Kiev over the legal status of the Autonomous Republic of Crimea have begun in 1991 and were executed in a serious of controversial legal actions on both sides. It culminated with the adoption of the Law on the Autonomous Republic of Crimea, by the Ukrainian parliament on March 17, 1995 and by constitutional definition of Sebastopol as a city under republican subordination on one side and with the adoption of the draft constitution of the Autonomous Republic of Crimea on November 1, 1995 on the other side.

The new constitution of Ukraine from June 1996 defines in articles 134 - 145 the status, competencies and functioning of the Autonomous Republic of Crimea. It prescribes among other the supervision of the Ukrainian parliament of the constitution of the autonomous republic. The constitution

---

[100]   Ibid.

[101]   Ibid.

[102]   The Federal Law on National-Cultural Autonomy has been adopted by the Duma on 22 May 1996, confirmed by the Council of the Federation on 5 June 1996 and promulgated by President Yeltzin on 17 June 1996. The law has six chapters and 21 articles. Source: The information library of the State Duma.

[103]   The Russian Duma has on May 23, 1992 adopted an act declaring the inclusion of Crimea in Ukraine in 1954 unlawful, and on July 9, 1993 reaffirmed the status of Sebastopol as a Russian city.

and other legal acts of the parliament of the autonomous republic and of its executive bodies as well must be in accordance with the constitution and legal order of Ukraine.

It is to be seen if the new constitution has definitely resolved at least some of political issues related to this sensitive geographical area. Still under discussion are also issues concerning the legal status of Crimean Tatars Medjlis (parliament) and of their representation in the Ukrainian and Crimea parliaments respectively. The Tartars were in 1944 massively deported from Crimea and have after 1989 returned in great number (about 300,000). The ethnopolitical situation in Crimea is characterised also by the existence of tensions between ethnic communities in general and between local administration and Crimean Tatars [104].

Transnistria The open ethno-political confrontation in Transnistria (Moldova) started when the Congress of the Transnistrian Soviets on September 2, 1990 adopted the "Decree on the State power in the Transnistrian Moldavian Republic" (TMR) and "The Declaration of Sovereignty of the TMR". These instruments were adopted following the Moldavian's Parliament adoption of "The Declaration on Sovereignty" and "Decision on the illegality of Bessarabia's annexation by the USSR" on June 28, 1940. The later act contributed to the speculations on the possible unification of Moldova with Romania what inhaled the requests of the Russian population of the eastern part of the country for independence. The armed conflicts terminated by political intervention from abroad - the latest being launched by the joint declaration by the presidents of Moldova, Russia and Ukraine on January 19, 1996 - and by mediation by two parts involved.

The contradictory legal actions exercised by two parts aimed at legalisation of their political positions culminated by the draft bill adopted by the Moldovian Parliament in January 1996 and by the alternative proposal of the authorities of Transnistria of the draft Agreement on the Joint Competencies of Transnistria and the Republic of Moldova [105]. The first document defines Transnistria as a territorial formation with the structure of an autonomous republic and with special status in conformity with the constitution and the law. Moldovian, Russian and Ukrainian are recognised as official languages of Transnistria.

The Republic of Moldova would retain the basic powers related with the statehood, and the local authorities of Transnistria would be responsible mainly for the supervision of existent legal, economic, financial and other enactment, for the creation of a municipal police force, for "solving problems" of health, social security, education, science, culture, sport, protection of environment, for "guaranteeing the activities of regional television and radio", and for "establishing and functioning of means of communication". Besides, Transnistria would participate in the foreign policy of Moldova when matters arise affecting its own interests, but shall also maintain international contacts in the economic, scientific and cultural spheres [106].

---

[104]   Serhiy Holovaty, Territorial Autonomy in Ukraine, The Case of Crimea, Council of Europe, European Commission for Democracy through Law, Strasbourg, 11 April 1996, CDL-UDLAU (96)7 Restricted, p.11.

[105]   Alexei Barbaneagra, The Situation in Moldova, Council of Europe, European Commission for Democracy through Law, Strasbourg, 11 April 1996, CDL-UDLAU (96) 1 rev., Restricted, p.9.

[106]   Ibid, p. 11.

Art. 1 of the draft Agreement proposed by the Transnistrian part declares that "the Transnistrian Moldovan Republic and the Republic of Moldova construct their relations on the basis of constitutional norms and mutual understanding". The constitutions of the two entities should not contradict the Agreement. They proposed also interactions as regards the armed forces, foreign policy, budget etc. on the basis of bilateral agreements [107]. The situation continues to be a source of instability and a danger for security in the region.

The Baltic republics

The Constitution of Lithuania of 25 October 1992 has adopted the political and juridique model of the Nation-state where is not space for any model of minority autonomy. It prescribes the national unity, sovereignty of people, the unity and indivisibility of the state territory, and Lithuanian as the official language. As to minorities it refers to "the citizens who belong to ethnic communities" who have the right to "develop their language, culture and customs" (art.37). The law has opened the possibility to establish in the framework of the Parliament commissions on ethnic minorities.

As to the Polish minority, two conventions of local deputies of Polish origin (12 May, 1989 and 1 June, 1990) elected a Co-ordinating Council as a legitimate body for the realisation of the declaration of "Polish National Territorial Self-Management". The motion that was not implemented was supported by the Polish Union in Lithuania and by the Polish deputies in the Parliament [108].

The Constitution of Latvia of 22 December 1991 in the framework of the rights and duties of the citizen prescribes the respect for "traditions and customs of the Latvian people and of national and ethnic groups living in Latvia", without describing what characteristics constitutes the difference between the two "traditions and customs". According to the law on the free development and the cultural autonomy of national and ethnic groups of 19 March 1991 has the minorities the possibility to nominate their representatives to the Consultative council of nationalities which has a seat at the Supreme Council.

Article 50 of the Constitution of Estonia of 28 June 1992 provided "ethnic minorities" with the right to "establish institutions of local autonomy". On this basis was on 11 November 1993 adopted the Law on the Cultural Autonomy of National Minorities. As similar law of 12 February 1925 this law (art.1) also consider as "national minority" the citizens "who maintain long-standing, firm and lasting ties with Estonia" and who "are motivated by a concern to preserve together their cultural traditions, their religion or their language which constitute the basis of their common identity." National minority cultural autonomy may be established by persons belonging to German, Russian, Swedish and Jewish minorities and persons belonging to national minorities with a membership of more than 3000 (art.2/2).

The principal objective of cultural autonomy shall be the organisation of education in the mother tongue and monitoring of the use of resources provided for this purpose, the establishment of cultural organisations and institutions, and the establishment and bestowment of funds, scholarships and awards for the promotion of minority culture and education (art.5/1). The members of minorities must be

---

[107]   Ibid, p. 12.

[108]   Irena Juozeliuniene (1996), Ethnic Identities and Inter-ethnic Relations in Lithuania. Paper presented at the 17th Conference Europe of Regions, Odessa, 20-22 September 1996.

registered, on the basis of personal application, in the National Register of National Minorities what is a precondition for the application for national minority cultural autonomy (art.7 and 8) [109].

Conclusions

The increasing incidence of ethnic dissent is but one manifestation, though one with far-reaching implications, of the widening gap between state and civil society. The concept of civil society expresses an effort to resist or limit the power of the state with a view to protect spheres of autonomy for the human person and a variety of social organisations and associations. The principle of pluralism and the principle of liberty are related to each other in the relationship between the human being, intermediate associations and the political order [110]. The lingering confusion and/or competition between 'civicness' and ethnicity in many parts of the region is one of the most significant differences between the civil societies in Central Europe and Western civil society [111].

In considering the issues related to the rights and status of ethnic minorities it is not to be, on the other side, forgotten that the autonomy regimes could convert the human rights movement's framework of protection of open inquiry and advocacy into the protection of static traditions. A state composed of segregated autonomy regimes would resemble more a museum of social and cultural antiquities than any human rights ideal. Enforced ethnic separation both inhibits intercourse among groups, and creative development within the isolated communities themselves. It impoverishes cultures and peoples [112].

The return to the roots, which is identified with cultural pluralism as an response to the homogenised culture of our mass societies, is thus only one side of the equation. The other side is equality of opportunity in a society which places a special premium on social mobility [113]. The equality in opportunity could be realised in the circumstances of economic and social development of the societies, what is not a case of many, especially Eastern-European societies. European integration will, of necessity, have to reconcile the acceptance of cultural diversity and linguistic pluralism with over-arching, shared values affecting such things as parliamentary democracy, freedom of the individual, social intervention, economic organisation, etc.

Autonomy remains a useful, if imprecise, concept within which flexible and unique political structures may be developed to respond to the increasingly complex interdependence of contemporary

---

[109]   Michael Geistlinger and Aksel Kirch (1995), Estonia: A new framework for the Estonian majority and the Russian minority (Wien: Braumueller, Ethnos, Bd.45).

[110]   Domingos Fernandes Gomes, The New Ethnic and Cultural Pluralism of European Society. Reflections at the Round Table, Notes et Documents, XV, 27/28, August 1990, p.22.

[111]   Dan Pavel, Civil society and security after communism. In: Chaillot Papers, ed.Ian Gambles. Institute for Security Studies, Paris, 1995, p.28.

[112]   See Henry Steiner, supra note, p. 1552-54.

[113]   J.Zubrzycki, Multiculturalism and the search for roots, Papers in multicultural studies (Centre for ulticultural studies, The Flinders University of South Australia, 1987), p.17.

world politics. The increasing frequency of claims to autonomy and the incremental effect such claims undoubtedly will have upon the international legal order make the concept of autonomy ripe for review.

The framework legal basis for the further improvement of the international legal order concerning ethnic autonomy represents the following: a. the notion of internal self-determination which could be interpreted as one of the rights emanating from art.1 of both Conventions on Human Rights of 1966, b. the "take part clause" of international law, c. the norms on political participation enshrined in art.21 of the Universal Declaration on Human Rights and in art.25.of the International Convention on Civil and Political Rights, d. the collective (cultural) rights of minorities which could be interpreted from the norm of art.27 of the ICCPR, e) the contents of art. 15 of the European Framework Convention on the Rights of National Minorities providing some kind of personal autonomy, f) the legal experiences of the European states in this field and g) the proposals of the NGO and other international expert groups. The improvement of regional and local self-government could be an adequate political environment for searching new incentives for ethnic autonomies. Subsidiarity in Eastern Europe could serve as an instrument in the national integration of geographically concentrated ethnic minorities. The application of the principle of subsidiarity to cultural and linguistic minorities, in short, could provide a useful vehicle in the continent and accommodation of counter-nationalist sentiment [114]. New legal norms and practical models of autonomy should be considered in the framework of the changing structure of the Nation-state and in the context of new dimensions of European integration.

---

[114] David Arter (1993), The Politics of European Integration in the Twentieth Century (Hants-Vermont: Darmouth Publishing House), p.274.

Mr Stanko NICK,
Member of the European Commission for Democracy trough Law

The activity of the European Commission for Democracy through Law in the field of minorities and local autonomy

The European Commission for Democracy through Law (the "Venice Commission") was established in 1990, at the initiative of the Italian senator, professor Antonio La Pergola, and by the resolution (90)6 of the Committee of Ministers of the Council of Europe of 10 May 1990.

It is an advisory body on constitutional law, set up with the purpose of assisting the Central and Eastern European countries, mostly countries in transition, in their constitutional reforms and to contribute to better harmonization of their legislation with the emerging European legal system. The Commission is available to contribute - without any obligation on the part of the requesting state - to the latter's legislative efforts, to help at the same time in better understanding of the European legal standards and, in the last instance, to facilitate and expedite the process of those countries becoming the members of the Council of Europe, of other European integrations and of closing the gap with industrially and socially most developed parts of the world. The Commission can also undertake general studies and propose draft laws or treaties. Apart from constitutional assistance and consultative functions in the preparation of fundamental legal instruments, the Commission has either on its own initiative or upon external requests, developed the sphere of its research and studies on important fields of legal questions connected with the functioning of democracy and its institutions, in both countries in transition and others.

From its first meeting the seat of the Commission has been in Venice, in the splendid 13th century building of la Scuola grande di San Giovanni Evangelista, put at the Commission's disposal four times a year, with generous assistance of Italian government, as well as that of Regione Veneto and the city of Venice itself.

The Commission is composed of individual, independent experts on constitutional and international law, from member states of the Council of Europe, as well as from non-member states. As the membership of the Council grows - my country is about to become its fortieth member - and as the activity of the Commission expands, both in geographical sense and in the way of substance, so is constantly increasing its composition. Presently some sixty members from more than fifty countries take part in the work of the Commission, as full members, associate members, co-opted members and observers. Strengthened by its considerable six years experience in the field of legal guarantees of democracy and numerous successful achievements in that period, the Commission's audience starts spreading outside Europe (including USA, Canada, Japan, Israel, South Africa, Armenia, Kyrgyzstan, Argentina, Uruguay etc), its sphere of investigation grows, the number of requests increase and they become more and more complex.

The Commission works in plenary and in sub-commissions. The number of those has gradually risen to ten: for constitutional justice, for federal and regional state, for international law, for protection of minorities, for constitutional reform, for democratic institutions, for South Africa, for Mediterranean basin, for emergency powers of the government, and for Latin America. Besides, the Commissions has a special research and education programme called UniDem (University for Democracy), conceived to focus on specific issues of particular interest from the point of view of development of democratic institutions and democratic practice. The programme includes the organization of seminars and preparation of follow-up publications, which provide a further contribution to the development of legal thought on democracy and the pre-eminence of law.

The Venice Commission has established its Documentation Centre on Constitutional Case-Law, which is becoming a significant computerised database for compiling and distributing important decisions taken by both European and non-European jurisdictions in the field of constitutional law and the protection of fundamental rights. A specialized publication, the *Bulletin on Constitutional Case-Law*, is printed regularly by the Centre. It is already a highly practical tool for the judges of constitutional courts, professors and students of constitutional law and anyone interested in following its evolution. It is envisaged to publish the electronic version of the Bulletin and as well to connect it to the Internet network.

The Commission co-operates closely with the statutory organs of the Council of Europe and its Secretary General, as well as with the Committee of Ministers, with the Parliamentary Assembly, with some Council of Europe Committees - such as Ad hoc committee on minorities (CAHMIN), Committee of experts on nationality (CJ-NA), Project Group "Human Rights and Genuine Democracy" (CAHDD), European committee on legal co-operation (CDCJ) and the Ad hoc Committee of legal advisers on public international law (CAHDI). It also co-operates with some other international organizations, among them the European Commission, the OSCE Office for democratic institutions and human rights , the OSCE High commissioner for national minorities, the UN High commissioner for human rights etc.

One of the main areas of interest of the Venice Commission is the protection of human rights generally, and the protection of the rights of minorities in specific. In that same context it pays considerable attention to the issues of federalism, new concepts of confederation, regionalism and local autonomy. Limited time and space allow us here to only review some of the Commission's endeavours and projects in this field, as example.

From the first year of its existence the Commission has been closely associated with the process of elaboration of the first pan-European instrument regulating this delicate issue, the Framework Convention for the Protection of National Minorities, 1995. It has also initiated the Proposal for a European Convention on the protection of minorities.

At the request of the Committee on Legal Affairs and Human Rights of the Assembly, the Commission gave its opinion on the possibility of identifying the provisions of the European Charter for Regional and Minority Languages which should be accepted by all contracting states. A similar request was made - and the opinion given - on the interpretation of the Draft Protocol on the rights of National Minorities to the European Convention on Human Rights, guaranteeing rights in the cultural field to persons belonging to national minorities (*Recommendation 1201/1993 of the Parliamentary Assembly*) and in particular Article 11 of this draft. This is the only text of the Council of Europe which deals with the issue of the right of the users of regional or minority languages to benefit from the establishment of local or regional authorities corresponding to the geographical area in which they live. The Commission gave its opinion on a number of minority protection or federal structure provisions in constitutions and national laws on minorities, such as those of Russia, Hungary, Croatia, Albania, Bosnia-Herzegovina.

The Commission has prepared a number of questionnaires seeking information from its members which would enable the undertaking of studies on various subjects connected with the area of reference. Such subjects were, among others: the Rights of minorities (in 1993), the Participation of persons belonging to minorities in public life (1996), Federal and regional states (1996). The replies were collected, examined and processed, and the results were published in full, in the series *Science and technique of democracy*.

In 1994 a UniDem seminar on Modern concept of confederation has been held in Santorini and the whole set of materials published afterwards in the collection of works. A UniDem seminar on "Local self-government, territorial integrity and protection of minorities" has very successfully been held in April 1996 in Lausanne. Several excellent papers were presented and they shall be available to the public as another volume in the collection *Science and technique of democracy*. Previously, a report on the Protection of Minorities in Federal and Regional States has been prepared and presented. The representative of the Commission participated at the Round table of experts on Federalism, held in April 1996 in Moscow.

Last but not least: when the Committee of Ministers examined the aptitude of Croatia for the admission to the Council of Europe, it produced a list of 21 conditions to be met and asked President of the Republic and the president of Parliament to guarantee its fulfilment. One of the conditions was to implement the recommendations resulting from the opinion of the European Commission for Democracy through Law in respect of the application of the Croatian Constitutional Law on the protection of human rights and the rights of minorities, as well as in respect of the protection of minorities by the Constitutional Court. A Working group has been established, and a very satisfactory result achieved. The result of which should be the admission of Croatia in less than a fortnight.

There is no doubt that these problems and the search for their best solutions shall for a long time remain in the focus of attention of the European Commission for Democracy through Law.

Prof. Peter KOVACS,
Lecturer, Deputy Head of Department, University of Miskolc, Law Faculty, Department of public international law (Hungary)

Participation of minorities in the management of local or national affairs concerning them in Hungary

The position of linguistic or ethnic minorities living in Hungarian territory

1. Pattern of minorities in Hungary: the problem of inaccurate data and the history behind it

Since the formation of the Hungarian state in the Carpathian Basin, the national population has always consisted of speakers of different languages, Hungarian being the most widespread. The enormous loss of life during the Turkish occupation and the war of liberation waged by the Holy League prompted the rulers, especially King Charles III and Queen Maria Theresa, to approve the idea of attracting large quantities of manpower chiefly from other parts of the Habsburg Empire and the lands remaining under Turkish rule. This measure, also applied in other feudal countries, placed the speakers of the various languages in inverse proportion. During the 19th century, the Magyar population found itself in the minority (between 42% and 48%) compared to the aggregate number of speakers of other languages.

The Trianon peace treaty (1920) took away two-thirds of Hungary's territory and gave the Magyar population a clear majority within the remaining area of 93,000 km². However, owing to the psychological consequences of the revisionist policy pursued between the world wars, the Nazi genocide, the deportation of the Jewish community in 1944, the partial expulsion of the German population after the war and the lingering effects of the anti-Tito stance adopted by Rákosi, the dictator from 1949 to 1956, it is very difficult to arrive at reasonably accurate figures for the breakdown of the population according to mother tongue or ethnic origin. There is deep distrust of censuses, and for their own self-preservation the persons surveyed often tend to conceal their true identities, one reason being that the 1941 census results furnished the legal basis for identifying the Germans who became eligible for expulsion after the war. (At the time, similar registers were used in Czechoslovakia and the USSR, but that was to identify the Hungarians who were stripped of their civil rights and collectively deported or expelled.) The recording of dual identities also raises certain technical problems.

It is interesting to observe the trends in the figures:

a.   according to the replies made to the nationality question in the 1980 and 1990 censuses:

- Germans: 11,310 (1980); 30,824 (1990)
- Slovaks: 9,110 (1980); 10,459 (1990)
- Croats, Slovenes or Serbs: 18,431 (1980)
- Croats: 13,570 (1990); Serbs: 2,905 (1990)
- Slovenes or others: 1,930 (1990)
- Romanians: 8,874 (1980); 10,740 (1990)
- Gypsies: 142,683 (1990)

b.   According to the replies made to the question on mother tongue:

-       Germans: 31,231 (1980); 37,511 (1990)
-       Slovaks: 16,054 (1980); 12,745 (1990)
-       Croats, Slovenes or Serbs: 27,052 (1980)
-       Croats: 17,757 (1990); Serbs: 2,593 (1990)
-       Slovenes or others: 2,627 (1990)
-       Romanians: 10,141 (1980); 8,730 (1990)
-       Gypsies: 48,072 (1990)

c.   Estimates by the government authorities on the basis of additional random sampling in 506 villages and towns (Hooz method):

-       Germans: min. 95,000
-       Slovaks: min. 50,000
-       Croats, Slovenes and Serbs: min. 38,000
-       Romanians: min. 10,000
-       Gypsies: 400-600,000 (overall estimate without sampling)

d.   Estimates by associations representing the interests of minorities:

-       Germans: 200-220,000
-       Slovaks: 110,000
-       Croats: 80-90,000; Serbs 5,000; Slovenes: 5,000
-       Romanians: 25,000
-       Poles: 10,000
-       Bulgarians: 3,000
-       Greeks: 2,500-3,000
-       Armenians: 1,500
-       Ukrainians: 451
-       Ruthenians (Rutheno-Ukrainians): 1,000
-       Gypsies: 600-800,000 or 1,000,000

2.   Legal and constitutional arrangements for minorities in Hungary

How are these highly diversified minorities to be secured proper and equal treatment?

In addition to provisions linking international and national law [1], or providing safeguards expressed in the European terminology of human rights [2], or in particular prohibiting discrimination [3], the Constitution enshrines the fundamental principles of effective participation by minorities in public life:

§68:
(1) The national and linguistic minorities in the Republic of Hungary shall share in the people's power, being constituent elements of the state.

(2) The Republic of Hungary shall accord protection to the national and linguistic minorities, ensuring their collective participation in public life, the cultivation of their culture, the use of their mother tongue, education in their mother tongue, and the right to use names in their own language.

(3) The laws of the Republic of Hungary shall guarantee the representation of the national and ethnic minorities living in the national territory.

(4) National and ethnic minorities may set up local and national self-governing bodies.

(5) The enactment of the law on national and ethnic minorities shall require a two-thirds majority of votes of members of parliament present.

---

[1] Article 7: The legal system of the Republic of Hungary shall accept the generally recognised rules of international law and shall ensure harmony between obligations under international law and the municipal law.

[2] Article 8: (1) The Republic of Hungary shall recognise fundamental human rights as inviolable and inalienable, and it shall be a prime duty of the State to respect and protect those rights. (2) In the Republic of Hungary, the rules relating to fundamental rights and duties shall be determined by law, which nevertheless cannot restrict the substance of any fundamental right.
Human rights are set out in Chapter XII (Fundamental rights and duties), Articles 54-70/K.

[3] Article 70/A: (1) The Republic of Hungary shall guarantee for everyone on its territory all human and civil rights without distinction of any kind such as race, colour, sex, language, religion, political or other opinions, national or social origin, property, birth or other status.

The Constitution laid particular stress on the institution of the ombudsman for minorities[4]. Quite plainly, the Constitution can regulate no more than the truly fundamental principles, and the specific conditions are established by separate legislation, notably the law on the rights of minorities. This law[5] passed in 1993 associates the concept of individual rights with a collective approach, expressed in "personal autonomy", as self-government is defined by a Hungarian authority on minority rights.

"Personal autonomy is a more difficult but at the same time more adequate solution to the problem of minorities", according to the writings of László Buza[6], a key figure in Hungarian international law doctrine who worked from 1910 to 1960. Mr Buza defined the third stage in the approach to the problem of minorities[7] as "guaranteeing through positive measures the fulfilment of

---

[4]   Chapter V: Parliamentary ombudsman for civic rights and parliamentary ombudsman for the rights of ethnic and national minorities.

Article 32/B. (1) The parliamentary ombudsman for civic rights shall have the duty to examine or have examined any irregularities brought to his attention in connection with constitutional rights, and to initiate general or individual measures to remedy them.

(2) The parliamentary ombudsman for the rights of national and ethnic minorities shall have the duty to examine or have examined any irregularities brought to his attention in connection with the rights of national and ethnic minorities, and to initiate general or individual measures to remedy them.

(3) Action by the parliamentary ombudsman for civic rights may be initiated by any person in the cases prescribed by law.

(6) The parliamentary ombudsman shall report annually on his activities to Parliament.

On election, cf:

Article 19: (3) Within its sphere of authority, Parliament (...)

(k) elects the President of the Republic, the Council of Ministers, the members of the Constitutional Court, the parliamentary ombudsman for civic rights and the parliamentary ombudsman for the rights of national and ethnic minorities, the President and Vice-Presidents of the State Audit Office, the President of the Supreme Court, and the Chief Prosecutor;

[5]   Law n° LXXVII of 1993 on the rights of national and ethnic minorities.

[6]   Buza, László: A kisebbségek jogi helyzete (The legal system relating to minorities) Magyar Tudományos Akadémia 1930 Budapest, p. 5.

[7]   He subdivised it into two systems, personal autonomy and territorial autonomy (idem).

the specific interests of minorities in such a way that - at least in certain well-defined spheres - state power is exercised separately on behalf of minorities as they intend, or possibly with their co-operation or, why not, by the minorities themselves."[8]

"Personal autonomy" theoretically makes it possible to apprehend those situations where territorial autonomy cannot be applied (because of the distances between municipalities populated chiefly by linguistic minorities or for want of compact settlement) and neither does local autonomy give complete satisfaction (as the solution to the problems of minorities in municipalities where the linguistic minority merely forms a local minority depends perforce on the local majority).

In fact the solution prescribed by Hungarian law only partially corresponds to this idea of "personal autonomy": institutions securing it are indeed provided for in the letter of the law, alongside and as it were above the normal institutions of local self-government, the individual rights of persons belonging to minorities and the collective rights pertaining to these minorities. It is the essential ingredient in a coherent complex of instruments. Logically, self-government, present at various levels of society, tends to be linked with collective rights. At the same time, as will be explained below, it embodies the applied principle of *subsidiarity*[9]. Even so, in theory self-government is also conceivable in the framework of the organisation of public administration [10] and not necessarily in the human rights framework. Nor indeed is it alien to human rights - Hungarian law can find landmarks in international practice: ombudsmen and Lapp assemblies in the Scandinavian countries [11] or certain Slovenian institutions (cf. opinion no. 7 of the *Badinter Commission*) [12]. At the same time, Hungarian law is consistent with the undertakings made in international law: the Council of Europe *European Charter for Regional or Minority Languages* [13] and bilateral treaties - which are furthermore based

---

[8]   Idem.

[9]   In the Council of Europe contribution to the CSCE Seminar in Warsaw (24-28 May 1993), it was stated that the application of the principle of local autonomy, naturally adapted to the diversity of situations, could prove a powerful factor both in the protection of minorities and in peaceful, civilised co-existence. The principle of subsidiarity mentioned in Article 4.3 of the Charter reads as follows: "Public responsibilities shall generally be exercised, in preference, by those authorities which are closet to the citizen."
        (HDSEMMIN III para.4)

[10]   In France, the Ministry of Education regularly concludes "agreements" with the Federation of Basque-Language Schools (SEASKA) embodying *inter alia* independent management of the budget allocated.

[11]   Article 3 of the "Basic Constitutional Charter" of 5 June 1991 , Article 64 of the Constitution, and Articles 5 and 81 secure to the Hungarian and Italian minorities a number of specific rights (right to their own national emblems, their national identity, right to a certain degree of political autonomy and minimum representation in the state or local bodies of the Republic, and right of veto in respect of legislation concerning the status of these minorities.

[12]   Article 3 of the "Basic Constitutional Charter" of 5 June 1991 , Article 64 of the Constitution, and Articles 5 and 81 secure to the Hungarian and Italian minorities a number of specific rights (right to their own national emblems, their national identity, right to a certain degree of political autonomy and minimum representation in the state or local bodies of the Republic, and right of veto in respect of legislation concerning the status of these minorities.

[13]   Hungary signed the Charter for Regional or Minority Languages on 10 November 1992 together with 10 other countries. At the time of ratification, the undertakings in Part III were made in respect of the Serbian, Slovenian, Croatian, German, Slovakian and Romanian languages.

on the individual as well as the collective approach to the protection of minorities, and establish bilateral supervision machinery [14] - are the frame of reference, supplementing the other stipulations of international law [15].

Self-government in terms of "personal autonomy" thus find its technical justification in the geographical distribution of minorities in Hungary. Its legal justification is inferred from the aforementioned stipulations of the Constitution and to some extent from the law on local authorities [16]; its political justification stems from the will of the minorities concerned -which conducted negotiations as a united front: the government had as its associate and talking-partner an *ad hoc* representative body made up of delegations of the interest [17] - and the meeting of minds between the government [18] and the parliament. (This is also expressed by the virtual unanimity [19] with which the law was passed). The long drafting procedure, in which the commencement and the first draft date back to 1989-90 [20], also testifies to the fact that the minorities regarded the proposals founded on traditional freedom of association [21] as inadequate.

Under the terms of the law, a national or ethnic minority is a community *(Volksgruppe)* in a numerical minority by comparison with the other inhabitants of the state, which has resided in the territory of the Republic of Hungary for at least a century, and whose members - who are Hungarian

---

Cf: Kovács, Péter: La protection des langues des minorités ou la nouvelle approche de la protection des minorités? (Quelques considérations sur la Charte européenne des langues régionales ou minoritaires) Revue Générale de Droit International Public No. 2/1993.

[14] Hungary-Ukraine: Treaty on good-neighbourly relations and foundations of co-operation (6 December 1991), Declaration on principles of co-operation in the protection of the rights of national minorities (31 May 1991) and Protocol thereto (31 May 1991).
Hungary-Slovenia: Treaty on good-neighbourly relations (1 December 1992) and Convention on the special rights of the Slovenian minority living in Hungary and of the Hungarian minority living in Slovenia (6 November 1992).
Hungary-Croatia: Convention on the rights of the Croatian minority living in Hungary and of the Hungarian minority living in Croatia.

[15] Article 27 of the International Covenant on Civil and Political Rights (1966), Article 14 of the European Convention on Human Rights (1950), the International Convention on the Elimination of All Forms of Racial Discrimination (1965), and the UNESCO Convention on the Elimination of Discrimination in Education (1960), etc.

[16] Law No. LXV (1990) on local authorities and Law No. LXIV on the election of local representatives for local authorities and of mayors.

[17] The "round table" of minorities.

[18] Mr Wolfart, Secretary of State and Head of the Office for National or Ethnic Minorities, was assigned responsibility for the inquiry in conjunction with the "round table of minorities".

[19] Parliament adopted it by 304 votes in favour, 3 against and 8 abstentions.

[20] That is, the final year of the reformist-socialist government in which Deputy Minister Tabajdi conducted negotiations and preparations in the framework of the College of National and Ethnic Minorities.

[21] Work in this connection was undertaken chiefly among the Ministry of Justice experts (during the 1989-90 phase as well as the 1990-1993 phase) and dealt with legislative alternatives. The College, and later the Office, accordingly opted for the principle of self-government.

citizens - differ from other population components in language, culture and traditions. According to this definition, evidently inspired by Mr Capotorti, the following communities are assumed to be traditionally settled in Hungary: Germans, Armenians, Bulgarians, Croats, Greeks, Poles, Romanians, Ruthenians, Serbs, Slovaks, Slovenes, Gypsies and Ukrainians.

Minorities as communities are entitled to establish their own forms of social organisation and autonomy at local and national level. They are entitled to the representation secured by the Constitution, the conditions of which are to be settled by the law on elections [22]. The Parliament has elected an *ombudsman* (mediator) to supervise and further the effective exercise of the rights of national or ethnic minorities.

The law recognises the creation and operation of minoritys' self-government - in the sense of cultural autonomy - as the most important requirement for minorities to assert their rights. It thus enables minorities in the municipalities, the towns and the districts of the capital to establish their own municipal councils or to bring into being, whether directly or indirectly, self-government bodies with a local or a national remit. A municipal council may declare itself a minority council if 50%+1 of its representatives have been elected as candidates in respect of a national or ethnic minority. Where at least 30% of the members of a local assembly have been elected as candidates in respect of the same minority, these may form a local minority council consisting of at least 3 members. (If the population is below 1,300, this body is constituted by 3 delegates. There are 5 in a municipality with a population of over 1,300. In towns there are 7, and 9 in towns which are county capitals and in districts of the national capital.) It is also possible to elect local self-government bodies directly by special local initiative. (Elections of this kind were held on 11 December 1994 in conjunction with the municipal elections and were also held additionally at the end of 1995 by central government decision.) Where the minority is unable to form a local minority council, its interests are represented by the ombudsman for minorities.

The respective powers of the various minority self-government bodies are defined as follows by the law, according to an official translation :[*]

§26:
1. Municipal minority councils and local minority councils may, in matters affecting the situation of minorities, refer to the head of the appropriate administration in order to:

a) request information;

b) submit proposals;

c) request the application of certain measures;

d) object to any practice or decision relating to the operation of institutions and violating minority rights, with a view to the modification or withdrawal of the decision in question.

2.   The head of the administration, in the cases defined in (1) above, must make a substantive reply to the appeal within 30 days.

---

[22]   The relevant part of the law on elections, however, did not gain the 2/3 majority. The Constitutional Court found an infringement of the Constitution by the legislator which will be analysed below.

[*]   Translator's note: AS/JUR (44) 24 = CDL-MIN (92) 1, reproduced with stylistic changes.

3.   If the head of the administration appealed to does not have competence or authority with respect to the subjects of the appeal, he shall refer the appeal within 3 days to a competent body.

§ 27:
Within their own sphere of competence and within the limits of the provisions made by the municipal council, the local minority council shall determine:

a)   its organisational and operational structure and its rules of procedure;

b)   its budget and final accounts and the use of resources allocated by the local council;

c)   the use of separate resources allocated to it from the resources of the municipal council in accordance with the provisions of the present law;

d)   the name, emblems and honours of the minority council and the regulations on their conferment;

e)   the local holidays of the minorities it represents;

f)   in accordance with the regulations pertaining thereto, the list of its protected monuments, commemorative sites and the local rules for their protection.

2.   On the initiative of the minority council, the representative body forming the municipal council shall determine the resources and assets which it is required to provide for the use of the minority council, itemising the movable and immovable assets and the financial resources, so that the minority council may discharge the functions defined by law.

3.   Within its sphere of competence, the minority council may found and operate as far as its resources permit institutions in the following areas in particular:

a)   local public education;
b)   local press and electronic media;
c)   maintenance of traditions;
d)   culture.

4.   Within the framework and limits assigned to it, the minority council may:

a)   found and operate enterprises or other economic concerns;
b)   organise competitions;
c)   establish scholarships.

5.   If a decision by the municipal council is required in order to enable the minority council to exercise its rights, the representative body shall place on the agenda of its next meeting the minority council's request for the necessary decision. Where the decision is in the remit of another self-government body, the latter shall take a decision within 30 days following the submission of the request.

§ 28:
The mayor's office, appointed by the municipal council, is required to render assistance in the proceedings of the local minority councils in accordance with its rules of procedure.

§ 29:

1.	For the purpose of enacting local by-laws on local public education, local media, maintenance of traditions and local culture and use of the language associated with the minority population's status as a minority, the representative body of the municipal council shall obtain the consent of the local minority council representing the minority population.

2.	The consent of the local minority council is required for the appointment of heads of minority educational institutions and for decisions concerning the training of members of minorities. In the absence of a minority council, an opinion shall be given by the ombudsman for the minority or, in his absence, by the local association of the minority.

3.	Whichever authority holds the right of approval and the right of inspection shall notify its decision within 30 days after receiving the request or being apprised of its content. Thereafter, these rights shall be forfeited.

§ 30:

1. Municipal and local minority councils may maintain relations with any other minority organisation or association and conclude co-operation agreements with them.

2.	Minority organisations, institutions and associations may enter state competitions conducted in the fields of culture, education and science on equal terms with minority self-government bodies.

§ 37:

The national minority councils, under the arrangements and within the limits established by law, shall decide independently on:

a)	seat, organisation and operation;
b)	budget, final account and property inventory;
c)	elements constituting its entire property;
d)	names and emblems;
e)	national holidays of the minorities which they represent;
f)	honours and conditions and rules for their conferment;
g)	principles and procedures for use of radio and television frequencies at their disposal;
h)	principles for use of the public service radio and television programme time at their disposal;
i)	release of press statements;
j)	foundation of institutions, their organisation and rules of procedure, upkeep and operation;
k)	foundation and operation of theatres;
l)	foundation and upkeep of museum or public collections constituted by collectors throughout the country.
m)	constitution of libraries for minorities;
n)	establishment and operation of an arts or science institute or a publishing company;
o)	maintenance of secondary and higher education establishments under national authority;
p)	provision and operation of a legal aid service;
(...)
r)	discharge of other duties assigned to them by law.

§ 38:

1. The national council

a)	expresses its opinion on draft laws affecting the minorities it represents as such, including decrees by the general assemblies of counties and the capital;

b)	may request information from administrative bodies on matters concerning groups of minorities they represent, submit proposals to them, and call for measures to be taken in matters within their competence;

c)	co-operates with the relevant state bodies in the professional supervision of primary, secondary and higher education for the minorities it represents.

(...)

3.	For the purposes of legislation on the maintenance of historical settlements, the consent of the national minority council - and of the local minority self-government bodies in the case of legislation concerning them - is mandatory.

If there is no local minority council, it is the spokesperson, or failing that, the local minority association, which gives its consent.

4.	With the exception of higher education, the national council has the right of approval as regards preparation of the general syllabus for the education of minorities.

§ 39:

Within its sphere of activity, the national council may organise competitions or establish scholarships.

§ 40:

(...) the local minority ombudsman is authorised:

a)	inasmuch as he is not a member of the local council's representative body, to be present in an advisory capacity at its meetings and those of all its committees, including closed sessions, dealing with questions concerning a minority;

b)	to propose to the mayor and to the committee chairman during council or committee meetings that a debate be held on any issue affecting the situation of minorities which comes within the remit of the council or committee;

c)	to initiate a review by the representative body of any decision by its committee concerning the situation of minorities;

d)	during meetings of the representative body or of its committee, to request information from the mayor, the clerk or the committee chairman on local government business of concern to minorities;

e)	to request from the mayor or the clerk such information and administrative co-operation as is necessary for the discharge of his duties;

f)	to request action by the mayor, the clerk or any official holding the appropriate responsibilities in matters affecting the minority as such;

g)	to propose that the representative body, in matters affecting a minority, turn to a state authority (...)

2.	Pursuant to the initiatives provided for in sub-section 1, paragraph (b), the mayor or the committee chairman shall submit the ombudsman's proposal to the next session of the representative body or the committee, which shall decide whether to place the issue on the agenda and what preparatory steps will be taken for its discussion.

3.	If the ombudsman requests information from the mayor, the clerk or the committee chairman during the session of the representative body or the committee, a substantive reply must be furnished either during the session or in writing within 15 days thereafter.

4.   On the ombudsman's request, his statement shall be included in the minutes of the session or - if submitted in writing - appended thereto.

5.   Discussion of the issue which affects the situation of minorities and has been placed on the agenda following an initiative as provided in sub-section 1, paragraph (b) and in accordance with the provisions of sub-section 2, cannot be postponed or removed from the agenda except at the ombudsman's request.

6.   Before issuing any decree determining the rights and obligations of a minority, or before taking measures which generally influence the situation of minorities, the municipal council shall consult the ombudsman.

§ 46:
     1. Municipal councils and local minority self-government bodies shall assist in assessing needs in respect of minority education and its organisation.

(...)

§ 47:
     Local minority self-government bodies may not take over from another body the control of educational establishments unless the standard of education hitherto achieved can be maintained. The extent of state support to these establishments cannot be reduced after the transfer of responsibility.

The combined municipal and minority elections in 1994 and the minority elections in 1995 yielded the following results:

| | Local or municipal minority self-government bodies | | Self-proclaimed municipal self-government body | | |
| | Directly elected | Indirectly elected | | Directly elected | |
	11 Dec. 94	11 Dec.94	11 Dec. 1995	19 Nov. 1995	Total
Bulgarian	2			2	4
Rome	415		1	61	477
Greek	2			4	6
Croat	35	1	15	6	57
Polish	2			5	7
German	98	7	19	38	162
Armenian	9			7	16
Romanian	9		1	1	11
Ruthenian	1				1
Serb	19				19
Slovak	28	4	6	13	51
Slovene	2		3	1	6
Total	622	12	45	138	817

A special chapter of the law settles matters concerning the administration of the freedoms secured to minorities and national support to them. In accordance with these provisions, the Parliament, following the entry into force of the law, set up the Fund for National or Ethnic Minorities in aid of minorities and activities carried out on their behalf [23].

The rules on use of the languages of minorities are modelled on the *European Charter for Regional or Minority Languages.*

---

[23]   During the first two years after the law's entry into force, the national budget is to provide a special compensation fund for minorities with an annual value of 0.5 billion forints. This will be used to cover the cost of establishing local and national self-government. In addition, a non-recurring grant of 300 million forints is prescribed to help selfgovernment for minorities started.

Why was such an intricate and highly (even unduly) complex arrangement chosen? The four "personifications" of local autonomy, namely municipal self-government, local self-government, the institution of the local ombudsman and national self-government, differ in purpose. **Municipal self-government** ("municipal minority council" in the law) is in fact an initiation into local autonomy in the European sense of the word. This can be practised in municipalities, where most of the electorate belongs to a minority.

The geographical distribution of minorities - as shown above - is such that some would be incapable of forming a local self-government body since generally speaking this would presuppose that the bulk of the local electorate [24] belongs to a national minority present only in some municipalities even in the case of the "principal" minorities.

Local minority self-government ("local minority council" in the law), however, caters for situations where the linguistic minority constitutes a minority even in the locality; apparently this type of institution could become far more widespread.

The local ombudsman is a special institution which operates when, despite the rules advocating positive discrimination, it has not been possible to elect even a local minority council [25].

National self-government ("the national minority council" in the law) is an elected body whose electors are persons working in the other self-government bodies [26]. Certain minorities may be unable to avail themselves of other forms of self-government than this national-level one, for want of a sound local basis.

As was observed above, the powers vested in the different forms of self-government are fairly similar and essentially concern the fulfilment of minorities' educational, cultural and traditional needs. This is where the two classic expressions of autonomy are apparent: either true self-government or co-decision (which in fact presupposes the right of veto). In other areas, the right to consult the local or state government bodies and the right to present them with initiatives are secured. The quality of the right of initiative is enhanced by the obligation of reply which is imposed on the body addressed.

Despite the complexity of the provisions, there is no duplication at local level because the three arrangements described above are alternative institutions whose actuation essentially depends on two factors: firstly the specifics of the geographical distribution of linguistic minorities, and secondly their political activism.

It was therefore expedient for the law to offer an array of instruments presenting a certain logical coherence and applying to the various minorities concerned while taking account of the wide numerical differences. *Subsidiarity*, ie devolution of powers, chiefly concerning matters of identity and culture and including the relevant budget, is practised at every level where self-government operates. Electoral legitimacy bolsters the responsibility of the representatives of minorities and at the same time

---

[24] Working on the assumption that the electorate follows the linguistic or ethnic preference.

[25] At the municipal elections, a candidate on an independent list for minorities who did not win a seat can hold office if he polls 2/3 of the number of votes gained by the candidate elected with the lowest score.

[26] That is, the members of the municipal minority council elected from the list of a minority, the members of the local minority council, and the ombudsmen. Where none of these operates in a given municipality, the appointment of a representative elector may be requested by three citizens claiming membership of the minority in question.

confers the duty of choosing between the various forms of organisation upon those directly concerned. In this way, it is also hoped to guard against government patronage.

As was explained above, one of the main technical problems is the lack of reliable data. The law - in its original wording -proposed the solution of an anonymous census based on the turnout at the municipal elections: using a special form [27] to be placed in a separate box from the ballot box, each voter could record his/her identity in privacy. By making appropriate statistical corrections [28], a more or less satisfactory figure could presumably have been worked out, and this would have helped secure due operation of the various forms of self-government. In 1994, however, at the call of minority interest groups, these provisions were repealed and so the anonymous census did not take place.

3.   The Constitutional Court and its case-law on minorities

The Constitutional Court has also furthered interpretation of the constitutional norms on the protection of minorities. Its chief pronouncements have borne on two issues: failure to observe the Constitution in enacting the law on the rights of minorities, and the problem of their parliamentary representation.

3.1   The Constitutional Court and the law on the rights of minorities

The enactment of this law was guaranteed by the Constitution (see above), but the Parliament elected in 1990 and Mr Antall's government restarted the consultations with the representatives of minority associations. For various reasons, these consultations and the experts' work went ahead rather slowly in the initial months. (It should be observed that the law was intended to be passed by Parliament with a 2/3 majority, and the Conservative coalition did not hold such a majority.) At that stage the (Socialist) member Tabajdi, former Minister for Minorities (1989-90), made a plea of unconstitutionality

---

[27]   Annex No. 3 to Law No. LXXVII of 1993

"Form for anonymous registration of membership of a national and ethnic minority

As a Hungarian citizen, of which national or ethnic minority or minorities do you consider yourself a member having regard to your mother tongue, the language used in your family, and the cultural values and traditions which you consider yours?

Bulgarian - Gypsy (Roma) - Greek - Croat - Hungarian* - German -Polish - Armenian - Romanian - Ruthenian - Serb - Slovak - Slovene - Ukrainian

If you belong to more than one minority, you may mark these accordingly. The information given concerning membership of a national and ethnic minority is in accordance with the provisions of Section 65 of Law No. LXXVII of 1993 on the rights of national and ethnic minorities. The above enumeration reproduces the list of national and ethnic minorities appearing in the text of the law.

The information given on this form will be processed anonymously in accordance with the provisions of Section 65 of Law No. LXXVII of 1993 and the provisions on the protection of personal and statistical data.

*   This option enables you to register as a member of the national majority and a national minority at the same time.

The writer devised this solution in 1989-90 for the College of national and ethnic minorities. At the time, the members representing the minorities did not see fit to include it. It was reintroduced in 1993 as an amendment by the Members of Parliament Tabajdi and Jakab.

[28]   Increased to allow for the local abstention rate, the absence of minors, etc.

110

to the Court for failure to enact the law in due time. The Court allowed the application but suspended its deliberations until 1 January 1992, granting the National Assembly an extension of time.

On 10 June 1992, since the law had not yet come into being, the Court found [29] that the legislator was at fault and set a final date on 1 December 1992. In the reasons for its decision, the Court referred to Article 68 of the Constitution and the deferral of Section 68 of Law No. LXV (1990) on local authorities and stated that *"representation is an absolute prerequisite for national and ethnic minorities to assert their position as constituent elements of the state."* The Court found that *"the institution of a general representation by the legislator has still not been effected according to the method and measures required by the provisions of the Constitution."*

3.2 The Constitutional Court and parliamentary representation of minorities

The other major decision of the Court was delivered in connection with the law on elections [30]. The law on the rights of minorities stipulated parliamentary representation of minorities, making reference to "a law". However, in order to amend the electoral law accordingly the Conservative coalition did not obtain the 2/3 majority despite the support of the Socialist Party which was then in opposition. The applicant asked that the law on elections be declared unconstitutional.

The Court declined to rule on the constitutionality of the law. It stressed that *"it is part of the legislator's freedom to choose whether it intends to legislate in one or a number of laws where legislation is mandatory."* Furthermore, in its decision the Court, referring to the aforementioned decision No. 35/1992 (VI.10) AB, drew attention to the fact that in the said decision it had not designated the law on elections as the sole possibility of ensuring representation.

The Court, after noting the partial fulfilment of the obligations deriving from decision No. 35/1992 (VI.10) AB through the enactment of the law on the rights of minorities, found that *"in the light of the foregoing, decision No. 35/1992 (VI.10) AB has already established the unconstitutionality of the failure to institute representation of minorities in the National Assembly."* Accordingly, the Court found that the application in the case before it was *res judicata* and on that ground refused to consider it on the merits.

In point of fact, nothing of the kind is explicitly set out in decision No. 35/1992 (VI.10) AB!

In that decision, as we have seen, the Court found that the failure to enact the law on the rights of minorities in due time infringed the Constitution and it made reference to the institution of general representation as a *sine qua non*. Theoretically, prior to decision Nº 24/1994(V.6) AB, one might have viewed the failure to secure parliamentary representation as a <u>plain</u> legislative shortcoming. Now it is evident that the national self-government structures for minorities will not satisfy the Constitutional Court.

One would even be inclined to say that the Constitutional Court has retroactively conferred constitutional force on the principle of guaranteed parliamentary representation of minorities.

It remains to be seen how this challenge will be met by the constitutional reforms for which the government has already commenced preparatory studies.

---

[29]   Decision No. 35/1992 (VI.10) AB.

[30]   Decision No. 245/1994 (V.6) AB.

4. Conclusions

Hungarian law is not a *cure-all* for solving *every* problem of the minorities, but rather an instrument which is designed to apply the *subsidiarity* principle and which presupposes activity or even activism on the part of the minorities themselves. However, the array of actual institutions at the disposal of a given minority basically depends on its objective situation - ie its territorial foundation - and its determination to realise the various forms of self-government.

It may be surprising to see such a short list of minorities in many cases, but it should not be overlooked that - as the Badinter Commission rightly pointed out, if a state contains one or more groups constituting one or several ethnic, religious or linguistic communities, these groups, by operation of international law, are entitled to have their identity recognised [31]. The abstract principle of self-government can furnish a host of practical solutions, and it puts into practice the adage that the right of self-determination is a principle safeguarding human rights. By virtue of this right, all persons can claim membership of the ethnic, religious or linguistic community of their choice [32]. The various activities will no doubt provide a sound basis for assessing proposed ways of representing interests.

Hungarian law is admittedly complicated indeed. Of course it does not provide the ideal solution as there is no ideal solution applicable to all contingencies at the same time. Having its place in the context of the other constitutional and international undertakings, it serves to validate the principle recognised as ***jus cogens*** by the Badinter Commission that states are required by the now peremptory norms of general international law to ensure that the rights of minorities are respected [33].

---

[31]   Opinion No. 2 para. 2.

[32]   Opinion No. 2 para. 3.

[33]   Opinion No. 2 para. 2,
Opinion No. 9 para. 2, and
Opinion No. 10 para. 4.

Prof. Nicolas LEVRAT,
Centre de droit public et de droit international de l'Université libre de Bruxelles,
Institut européen de l'Université de Genève, Membre du bureau d'Arcole

Text introducting the round table on minorities and transfrontier co-operation in Europe

Transfrontier cooperation is a relatively recent phenomenon in international relations which allows infra-governmental public bodies to participate in international relations, through specific machinery, in their own sphere of activity, distinct from both intergovernmental international law and from relations between individuals in an international context. In Europe, a pioneering continent in the field, there is a legal framework for transfrontier cooperation developed by the Council of Europe. The *European Outline Convention on Transfrontier Cooperation between Territorial Communities or Authorities* (1980), Article 10 para.3 of the *European Charter of Local Self-government* (1985) and the *Framework Convention for the Protection of National Minorities* (1995) form the legal foundations for this framework.

The recognition and protection of the rights of minorities emerged within the great multi-nation empires (the Austro-Hungarian Empire, the Ottoman Empire) that no longer exist today. As these empires disappeared after the First World War, a body of international law on minorities took shape, inspired primarily by the American President, Woodrow Wilson. Modern international law, however, which has risen from the ashes of the Second World War, has been slow to produce specific texts for the protection of minorities, preferring the concept of universal protection of human rights [1]. It was not until the upheavals in Europe in 1989 that a fresh impetus was given in Europe to developing instruments for the protection of minorities. Thus, in 1995, a *Framework Convention for the Protection of National Minorities* was opened for signature in the Council of Europe.

In these two fields - one relatively new, the other "dusted off" after a long period in storage - the legal instruments providing for the implementation of transfrontier cooperation and those on the protection of minorities are both found among the European Treaties drawn up by the Council of Europe. Is this sufficient to warrant combining these two fields of law, when they are apparently so distinct? The first is clearly connected to the development of member States' administrative structures and is the consequence of enhanced cooperation between these States for the purpose of achieving

---

[1]   In this respect, Resolution 217 (III) C adopted by the United Nations' General Assembly clearly establishes the principle of the supremacy of the universal protection of human rights over the development of a body of law specific to minorities.

113

greater unity, in which there is a wish to include local and regional authorities [2]. The second field, on the other hand, belongs wittingly to the human rights domain [3].

These differences in category, which may give legal experts food for thought, do not appear to have stopped European decision-makers from drawing a link between the instruments in the two fields. The Heads of State and Government of the Council of Europe member States, meeting at the Vienna Summit on 9 October 1993, adopted in an Appendix to the Final Declaration a text on national minorities which they concluded by instructing the Committee of Ministers (of the Council of Europe) "to respond to requests for assistance for the negotiation and implementation of treaties on questions concerning national minorities as well as agreements on transfrontier cooperation" [4]. This link drawn explicitly by the Heads of European States may appear, having regard to the wording of the paragraph in question, fortuitous or at the very least somewhat artificial. The reader is aware that a possible link exists but that the reference to transfrontier cooperation has just been added as an afterthought, a suggestion which appears to make sense but from which the authors themselves have not drawn all the conclusions.

This first link is followed by two provisions from the *Framework Convention for the Protection of National Minorities* which, in much more explicit terms, grant a right for people belonging to national minorities to cooperate across frontiers. Article 17 of the *Framework Convention* states that :

"The Parties undertake not to interfere with the right of persons belonging to national minorities to establish and maintain free and peaceful contacts across frontiers with persons lawfully staying in other States, in particular those with whom they share an ethnic, cultural, linguistic or religious identity, or a common cultural heritage."

---

[2]   The preamble to the *European Outline Convention on Transfrontier Co-operation between Territorial Communities or Authorities* (European Treaty Series no. 106) opens with the following words :

"The member States of the Council of Europe, signatories to this Convention,

Considering that the aim of the Council of Europe is to achieve a greater unity between its members and to promote co-operation between them;

Considering that, as defined in Article 1 of the Council of Europe Statute, this aim will be pursued in particular by agreements in the administrative field;

Considering that the Council of Europe shall ensure the participation of the territorial communities or authorities of Europe in the achievement of its aim;"

[3]   Article 1 of the *Framework Convention for the Protection of National Minorities* reads as follows : "The protection of national minorities and of the rights and freedoms of persons belonging to those minorities forms an integral part of the international protection of human rights, and as such falls within the scope of international co-operation."

[4]   Appendix II to the *Vienna Declaration* of 9 October 1993.

This article, which serves as the principal legal basis for analysing, as we are doing here, the links between the issue of minorities and transfrontier cooperation, calls for certain remarks. But we should stress first of all that it is no surprise to find here, albeit in more developed form, the path marked out in Appendix II to the *Vienna Declaration* of 1993, since the *Framework Convention for the Protection of National Minorities* originated in that same appendix, in the paragraph following the one linking transfrontier cooperation and national minorities.

However, this article does not refer to the machinery proper to transfrontier cooperation which, as suggested by the title of the 1980 Outline Convention, must be implemented by territorial communities or authorities, in other words by public bodies and not by individuals. Article 17 on the other hand applies only to individual rights, the right of each person belonging to a national minority and not the right of the national minority itself, nor that of a group representing the interests of the individuals belonging to a national minority - for example, following democratic elections. This fundamental difference is explained chiefly by the conceptual and practical difficulty that exists in the branch of law dealing with human rights in conceiving collective rights [5].

This conceptual difficulty and its consequences for the wording of article 17 are not however insurmountable obstacles for our analysis. The Framework Convention does not confer any rights for specific forms of transfrontier cooperation on people belonging to national minorities - which would then be very difficult to exercise as individual rights - but simply prohibits States parties from obstructing transfrontier contacts by persons belonging to a national minority. It is therefore no more than a requirement by signatory States not to discriminate against people belonging to a national minority in their efforts to maintain transfrontier contacts, either individually or through a representative body, which may mean through a territorial community or authority [6]. In this way, the Framework Convention resorts in this specific field of contacts across frontiers - to use the words of article 17 - to the most traditional means that human rights law has to protect minority rights, namely the principle of non-discrimination.

The result is a reference to the common rules applicable in the field. As far as contacts between individuals are concerned, these come under various individual freedoms [7] which do not concern us here; however, if such contacts were to be made by territorial communities, then the principle of non-discrimination refers to the common rules applicable in the field, namely those on transfrontier cooperation. The Framework Convention, without producing the lengthy reasoning we have set out here, nevertheless holds the same position and provides in Article 18 paragraph 2 that "where relevant, the Parties shall take measures to encourage transfrontier cooperation". Here again, the wording of

---

[5]   In this respect, the comments on articles 1 and 3.2 of the *Framework Convention for the Protection of National Minorities* contained in paragraphs 31 and 37 of the explanatory report are quite explicit on the concern of the Convention's authors not to confer "collective rights" on minorities.

[6]   Without prejudging the interpretation a court might give to this provision, it seems quite conceivable that an individual could cite it if a territorial community to which he belongs, or of which he is an elected representative, has been obstructed in an act of transfrontier cooperation because persons from a national minority within the meaning of the *Framework Convention for the Protection of National Minorities* are part of its community.

[7]   For example, freedom of movement, freedom of information and freedom of association or assembly.

the provision does not define a specific form of transfrontier cooperation recognised by the Framework Convention for the protection of national minorities. Firstly it does not determine the holder of a particular right, and is therefore certainly not a directly applicable provision, unlike Article 17. Secondly, it is at best a reference to the albeit embryonic rules in the legal instruments drawn up by the Council of Europe in the field of transfrontier cooperation.

1.   The origins of transfrontier cooperation

Once this title has been developed, I should like to consider the use, on the basis of the criteria of Article 17 which seem more operational than those of Article 18.2, of transfrontier cooperation machinery for the purpose of developing transfrontier contacts between:

i)   people belonging to the same national minority and residing in different States, or
ii)   people belonging to a national minority on one side of the border and others belonging to the "mother nation" the other side of the border, or
iii)   people belonging to different national minorities either side of an international border, or
iv)   people belonging to a national minority and others belonging to a territorial community abroad.

Article 17 was most certainly worded to cover relations in the first three categories, and probably mainly the first two since it specifies that these contacts across frontiers concern "in particular" people belonging to a national minority who "share an ethnic, cultural, linguistic or religious identity". This fits into a general pattern. If we look at the reasons behind the emergence of transfrontier cooperation, it can be seen that it is usually territorial communities located either side of an international border which share interests and have common problems or needs, that set up cooperation of this kind. Moreover, the peripheral location of such communities, near international borders and therefore generally - with exceptions in some countries [8] and a different case for small States - far away from national decision-making centres, has prompted them to turn to foreign partners which are closer at hand and easier to reach, despite the existence of an international border [9].

This situation is often that experienced by national minorities finding themselves, following the redefinition of national boundaries at various times in Europe's history (and particularly central Europe), confined close to the international borders of the State in which they live. Also, they are frequently marginalised, not only because of their geographical location but also because of their cultural, linguistic, religious or other differences. Lastly, there are often groups of people who share either the same situation (the same national minority or a different one the other side of an international border), or cultural, linguistic, religious or other characteristics which marginalise the members of the national minority in their country of residence (this would be the case of the mother nation).

As far as the origins of transfrontier cooperation are concerned then, in many cases enough parallels can be drawn with the situation of minority groups that a similar approach, satisfying

---

[8]   Some national capitals are relatively close to an international border, as is the case of Vienna, Bratislava, Helsinki and Tallinn.

[9]   For a survey of the development of such relations, see N. LEVRAT, *Le droit applicable aux accords de coopération transfrontalière entre collectivités publiques infra-étatiques*, P.U.F., Paris, 1994, pp. 21-39.

comparable needs, could be considered appropriate and could lead to the development of contacts across frontiers.

2. The original objectives of minorities law

It is with regard to this specific point that the idea of using transfrontier cooperation machinery as a possible means of satisfying the legitimate aspirations of national minorities might be the hardest to conceive. This could be regarded as a Copernican revolution in contemporary law on minorities compared with the conception of minorities law - which we should describe as Aristotelian if we were to maintain the metaphor - that prevailed between the two world wars in Europe. One of the fundamental aims of the Society of Nations - or the Versailles system - is to place the protection of national minorities in a framework of multilateral international relations so as to guard against the potential threat to Europe's political and military stability posed by the intervention of the "mother nation" to protect the members of "its" national minority. Thus any exercise in minorities law consisted in preventing such minorities from turning to the neighbouring State, to whose national community they belonged, in order to have their rights protected and respected; it was therefore decided to place this issue under the guarantee of the powers [10].

Is contemporary law on minorities today reversing this trend by encouraging minorities to maintain direct relations with a neighbouring State? It is not impossible since Article 18 paragraph 1 of the *Framework Convention for the Protection of National Minorities* encourages neighbouring States in particular to conclude bilateral and multilateral agreements [11].

However, article 18 paragraph 2, mentioned earlier, refers to transfrontier cooperation machinery, and hence to its specific aspects, and offers a solution that does not rely on bilateral relations between States, since transfrontier cooperation does not consist of relations between States but relations between infra-governmental communities, which firstly are not part of general international law - since territorial authorities are not subject to international law - and secondly do not raise matters of sovereignty as do intergovernmental relations.

---

[10]   For a brief description of these mechanisms, see for example S. BARTSCH, "Le système de protection des minorités dans la Société des Nations", in *L'Europe centrale et ses minorités: vers une solution européenne?*, P.U.F., Paris, 1993, pp. 37-50, or I. SCHULTE-TCHENCKHOFF and T. ANSBACH, "Les minorités en droit international" in *Le droit et les minorités*, Bruylant, Bruxelles, 1995, pp. 26-30.

[11]   In addition to the fact that this is a reversal of the historical perspective of minorities law, the researcher might be justified in questioning the compatibility of the use of bilateral agreements for "the protection of persons belonging to the national minorities concerned" and with proclaimed inclusion of this new minorities law in the international protection of human rights (see note 3 above for the text of Article 1 of the *Framework Convention for the Protection of National Minorities*). The fact is that the international protection of human rights is based on the principle of the universality of human rights (from which is derived, among others, the principle of non-discrimination which is the main guarantee in the human rights system for people belonging to minority groups); that universality will have little room for bilateral agreements aimed at protecting the minorities concerned (it is likely that the implementation of such agreements would lead to discrimination - for example against people belonging to minorities other than the "minorities concerned" - that is incompatible with the founding principles of the international protection of human rights). This question, which we consider to be of fundamental importance, cannot unfortunately be discussed in the limited scope of this article.

3.   Transfrontier co-operation machinery

As we have already stressed in the introduction, this machinery was introduced to allow the territorial authorities of the Council of Europe member States to maintain relations directly among themselves, while bearing in mind that these authorities are not subjects of international law and do not therefore have access to the machinery of international law [12]. Moreover, the rules governing such relations take account of the fact that the partners in transfrontier cooperation are public authorities and that they cannot therefore use machinery applying to relations between individuals, without running the risk of losing some of their specific characteristics as public bodies. These characteristics, which have shaped the development of legal rules capable of governing transfrontier cooperation define a strict framework which, given that the machinery will be applied to questions concerning the existence of national minorities, may be regarded as an advantage.

Firstly, transfrontier cooperation in the strict sense of the term can be developed only between infra-governmental public authorities. The relations between an authority of this kind and a foreign State fall outside this context and are therefore not covered by this machinery [13]. This resolves a delicate issue in the context of the protection of national minorities, namely the risk of intervention by a State (the "mother nation") in the affairs of a neighbouring State, on the pretext of safeguarding the protection of a national minority. This means that transfrontier cooperation machinery cannot serve as a "Trojan horse" for the interference of another State, since only territorial authorities or communities can engage in transfrontier cooperation. The legislation of several central and eastern European States which provides for prior approval from the Foreign Affairs Ministry for transfrontier cooperation agreements concluded by territorial communities in their country could have direct implications for the other State concerned, and thus render inoperative the transfrontier cooperation machinery in its aspects which concern us here.

---

[12]   On this point and its consequences, see N. LEVRAT, *op. cit.*, pp. 291-300.

[13]   This is quite clear from the wording of article 2 of the *European Outline Convention on Transfrontier Co-operation between Territorial Communities or Authorities* which defines transfrontier cooperation as "any concerted action designed to reinforce and foster neighbourly relations **between territorial communities or authorities** within the jurisdiction of two or more Contracting Parties ..." (our emphasis). Article 10 para. 3 of the *European Charter of Local Self-government* talks of local authorities "cooperat[ing] with their counterparts in other States" which, without limiting cooperation to other local authorities, nevertheless rules out central governments, which cannot be regarded as "counterparts" ("*collectivités*" in the French text) of local authorities.

Secondly, Europe's States consider transfrontier cooperation to be limited strictly to relations between neighbours [14]. This limitation, in the specific case of a territorial community representing the interests of a minority group, can also offer a guarantee that this direct cooperation will not cover issues other than local ones and interests concerning relations between neighbours on an international border.

Thus the limits imposed by the specific legal characteristics of the partners in transfrontier cooperation can, when such machinery is used by communities representing the interests of a minority group, act as obstacles to prevent such cooperation from being used to achieve aims other than the primary aim, and constitute a form of interference by a foreign state.

To conclude, we need to consider whether transfrontier cooperation machinery can be useful for minority groups

Existing texts to date are not quite clear as to how the issue of minorities and "transfrontier cooperation" is to be understood. It could be imagined that the aim of applying transfrontier cooperation machinery to minorities as such would be precisely that mentioned in the title of this section. As interesting as it may be, this approach is not currently envisaged, partly because the recognition of rights of this kind for minorities would amount to the recognition of "collective rights" for minorities, a principle which many Council of Europe member States would find difficult to accept. It should be stressed however, if we maintain a strict parallel with the rules of transfrontier cooperation, that the content of these rights would not be specified; reference would be made, instead, to domestic law to define the powers responsible [15]. This method would imply that such communities had already been recognised at national level and their responsibilities defined in domestic law. However, the practical difficulties relating in particular to the membership of the minority that would hold such rights mean that, as things stand, this hypothesis remains a Utopian ideal.

---

[14]   The Italian Government, for example, when it deposited its instrument of ratification of the *European Framework Convention on Transfrontier Cooperation* declared that the depth of the area within which Italian territorial entities were authorised to conclude the agreements and arrangements referred to in the Convention was 25km from the frontier, unless those entities bordered directly with a foreign State. Moreover, there are instruments and specific terminology covering transfrontier relations between infra-governmental public bodies which are not confined to neighbouring areas. Such relations are referred to as interregional or interterritorial (there is, for example, a preliminary draft Convention on interterritorial cooperation between territorial communities or authorities, *Resolution 248*(1993) of the CLRAE).

[15]   Thus Article 1 of the *Additional Protocol to the European Outline Convention on Transfrontier Co-operation between Territorial Communities or Authorities* states that "Each Contracting Party shall recognise and respect the right of territorial communities or authorities under its jurisdiction and referred to in Articles 1 and 2 of the Outline Convention to conclude transfrontier co-operation agreements with territorial communities or authorities of other States **in equivalent fields of responsibility**, in accordance with the procedures laid down in their statutes, [...]" (our emphasis).

However, if transfrontier cooperation machinery exercised by the partners initiating transfrontier cooperation - i.e. territorial communities or authorities - is regarded as offering the solution contained in the phrase "minorities and transfrontier cooperation", this raises a whole set of problems. Firstly, as has already been mentioned, the rights as defined in the *Framework Convention for the Protection of National Minorities* are rights which may only be held, and probably exercised, by "persons belonging to national minorities", even though they may exercise these rights and freedoms "individually as well as in community with others", as stipulated in article 3 paragraph 2 of the Convention. At the same time, the right to transfrontier cooperation concerns undeniably territorial communities and authorities, according to Article 1 of the *Framework Convention for the Protection of National Minorities*, or local authorities according to article 10 para. 3 of the *European Charter of Local Self-government*. It is therefore not easy to imagine how rights belonging to individuals can be exercised by territorial communities, even though an argument - which would require lengthy theoretical explanations that would nevertheless be interesting, albeit in a different context - based on the principles of representative democracy might produce a convincing conclusion.

Moreover, it is important to stress that area-based institutional solutions [16] to the issue of minorities, although they provide in certain circumstances a *de facto* response to the legitimate aspirations of a minority group, because the political structures (in this case, territorial communities) and the geographical location of the members of the minority coincide, are not legal solutions applying directly to the minorities as such [17]. Faced with this difficulty, we need to imagine transfrontier cooperation machinery that is for use not exclusively by territorial authorities or communities, but also by non-territorial communities representing minorities.

A solution of this kind is not only possible, but it has been implemented in a European country, namely Belgium. The linguistic communities, which are, at least in theory, non-territorial entities [18], are authorised by the Belgian Constitution to enter into international cooperation in the fields of culture and education (article 127 § 1, No 3 of the Belgian Constitution) and person-related matters (*"personnalisables"*) (article 128 § 1 of the Belgian Constitution). It is true that in practice,

---

[16] The same applies to other area-based solutions such as federalism, regionalism or local self-government, which are the main themes of this Conference.

[17] It is unlikely that an individual who forms parts of a minority group but who does not reside in the territorial community authorised to exercise transfrontier cooperation in the interests of the minority group to which he belongs, would be able to claim to benefit from the results of that transfrontier cooperation.

[18] In actual fact, the *Cour d'arbitrage* has more often than not placed the principle of territoriality, on which the regions are based, above that of a community of people, which the linguistic communities would appear to be, according to the letter of the law. This position, however, is based essentially on the concern to avoid conflicts between the country's two main linguistic communities when regulations enacted by virtue of a power exercised by a community conflicts with a regulation produced by a region, by virtue of its territorial powers. In the field of transfrontier - or international, as is the case with Belgium - relations, such disputes seems less likely to arise and the communities entertain relations which, it would seem, can benefit all the members of the community, membership of which would be based on person-related criteria.

the non-territorial base of the communities - or alternatively their composition on a person-related basis - has been seriously called into question.

We consider however that if transfrontier cooperation - which offers the major advantage of blending into international relations without encroaching on international law *stricto sensu* - were to be accessible to a degree to minorities, then it would have to be accessible to non-territorial entities (the minorities). It is therefore regrettable that the Council of Europe's texts on transfrontier cooperation refer exclusively to territorial communities. For our part, we prefer the broader term - which would have no implications from a legal point of view since the fields in which the communities are authorised to undertake transfrontier cooperation are defined by the powers assigned to them by domestic law - of **infra-governmental public community** [19] which could cover non-territorial entities. Such an extension of the field of application of regulations on transfrontier cooperation could certainly make an original and most probably useful contribution, allowing a direct link between the rights of minorities and transfrontier cooperation. This would pose no technical difficulties, as far as transfrontier cooperation was concerned. However, the question of defining the minority and how its rights are to be exercised - undoubtedly one of the central issues in minorities law - clearly remains unanswered.

As this brief study has shown, the paths opened by the juxtaposition of transfrontier cooperation machinery and issues relating to minorities appear to lead to fertile plains. Once these have been reached, the lawyers and experts who meet regularly in the Council of Europe will not fail to sow the seeds needed to add new shoots to the burgeoning field of minorities law.

---

[19] See our work, cited above in note 9, especially pp. 5 to 7 and 147 to 149.

Mr Ivan IAKOVCIC,
Istrian Region

Istria : a transfrontier co-operation project

The nation-state is a special socio-political structure combining a given territory, economic system, language, history and culture, that is to say a system dominated by the principles of internal homogeneity at all socio-cultural levels.

The nation-state model is very noticeably under attack in many parts of the world, especially where major language and culture groups meet and intermix. The systems of social interdependence and political organisation in such areas do not coincide with the linguistic and cultural boundaries.

The problem of national minorities in Europe becomes particularly critical when we attempt to apply the principles of democracy, nationality and national self-determination to realities in central and eastern Europe, with its enormous variety of ethnic groups.

However, the protection of individual rights will remain a legal dead letter if we disregard the social processes which generate and maintain de facto discrimination. This is why, in the name of pluralism, we must protect not only individuals but also groups.

One of the most interesting signs of this phenomenon today is regionalism, because there is a powerful alliance between the advocates of regionalism and those striving to protect ethnic groups and national minorities.

The "regional state" is a very valid alternative, as it has no claims on sovereignty and is therefore no mere variant of federalism; nor is it a variant of the 19th-century conception of the unitary state, because it generates a complex system of local self-governing institutions. Regionalism is at once the official recognition of a given country's profound territorial and local diversity and the result of reactions against the centralising state.

Regionalism is thus the natural ally of defenders of the principle of protecting minority ethnic groups. Obviously, therefore, national minorities can only welcome the decentralisation of political power to smaller territorial units in which they are not only numerically but also psychologically stronger, since in general (and in the specific case of Istria) a territory also implies contact between and overlapping of, cultures and the creation of common points of reference, which facilitate understanding and coexistence.

In ethnic terms, Istrians can identify with one or more of the three national groups represented in their region: Croatians, Italians and Slovenes. There is also the specific Istrian ethnic component. Their mother tongue may be one or more of the standard languages, which are Croat, Italian and Slovene, a dialect of one of these languages or a combination of any of the latter.

Accordingly, the first step in any transfrontier co-operation project in Istria must be to induce Croatia and Slovenia to decentralise their government departments as far as possible in accordance with the following principles:

1. The state shall recognise and promote local self-governing institutes, do its utmost to decentralise departments coming under its authority and tailor its legislative methods and principles to the requirements of self-government and decentralisation;

2. The state shall protect indigenous ethnic and linguistic minorities by means of appropriate legislation and regulations;

3. The state shall be divided into regions and municipalities;

4. Regions shall be set up as self-governing entities with independent powers and duties;

5. Istria, as a geographically and culturally unique and indivisible region, should be granted special forms and conditions of self-government, set out in a special statute enshrined in constitutional laws.

There are three primary reasons why transfrontier co-operation is needed in Istria:

1. Istrian citizens are expressing a clear need and desire to communicate freely and develop economic, cultural and other relations unhampered;

2. Transfrontier co-operation in Istria will enable the Republics of Croatia and Slovenia to act as links with the European institutions through either their state institutions or their regional and local authorities;

3. The Istrian transfrontier co-operation model, which is based on the multiethnic and multilingual nature of Istria, would consolidate the principle of the inviolability of state borders and increase the stability of European security structures.

Istria is an historic European region whose main features are a multiethnic environment and inter-ethnic tolerance. The inhabitants of the Slovene and Croatian parts of Istria voted respectively for the independence of the Republic of Slovenia in the plebiscite and the independence of the Republic of Croatia in the referendum organised on the subject. The novel situation in the territory of Istria, which is now divided up between three different states, has created the need for novel solutions to the problem of free communication among the citizens.

The political forces governing both the Croatian and Slovene parts of Istria are concentrating on finding ways of guaranteeing the well-being of citizens, the protection of human and minority rights, and the overall security of the territory. Work is currently proceeding on the planned transfrontier co-operation project based on the Outline Convention on Transfrontier Co-operation and the wide experience of such co-operation in the various European states.

The reasons for introducing transfrontier co-operation in Istria are as follows:

1. Istria is a unique multiethnic and multilingual territory, and any attempt to divide it destroys its identity as a European region which has grown up over the centuries. The fact that Croats, Slovenes, Italians and other ethnic groups in Istria have always lived in harmony and mutual tolerance is a cogent reason to overcome the present barriers on the basis of the European models.

If we acknowledge the right to be different, to belong to different ethnic groups and to use different languages and dialects in the territory of Istria, we will create and bolster a strong regional identity. This would enable Istria to provide its own specific contribution to the great European family.

2.   The Italians, as an indigenous national community in Istria, were divided up when the two nation-states of Croatia and Slovenia were founded. Many of the Italian community's institutions (eg the television corporation) are now in Slovenia, while others (such as the Historical Research Centre) are in Croatia. The appropriate mechanisms are therefore needed to prevent this group from being assimilated, as this would destroy part of the Istrian identity.

Considering that the nation-state framework is too narrow to solve all the problems of modern society, while on the other hand being too broad to solve problems which citizens can deal better with at a lower administrative level, regionalism is emerging as the cornerstone of a united Europe. The setting up of transfrontier regions is the epitome of regionalism and the concept of a united Europe because it respects the sovereignty of the individual states and overcomes borders rather than altering them.

Anyone discussing this subject in our country is open to attacks by various political forces, but the final outcome of such a policy and the support we are receiving from Europe show that we are fighting for a just future for both Istria and Croatia. This gives us the courage to fight on.

Mr Claude HAEGI,
President of the Congress of Local and Regional Authorities of the Council of Europe

Closing Speech

Ladies and Gentlemen,

Sharing views and pooling experience is an invaluable aid to problem-solving, and this has certainly been the case here in Cividale. The crucial issue is finding the right balance between the will of the majority and the aspirations of minority groups. Minorities' legitimate aspiration to autonomy and self-determination must find appropriate structures if it is to become a reality of everyday political life.

Mr Martini and Mr Albanese have already outlined the achievements of the Congress and the Council of Europe with regard to conventions on autonomy and minorities.

But before the conference ends I would like to discuss two practical initiatives taken by the Congress of Local and Regional Authorities of Europe which make a very positive contribution towards solving the problems of minorities highlighted during the conference. I am referring to the draft European Charter of Regional Self-Government and the "local democracy embassies".

At the 1993 Geneva Conference on the evaluation and perspectives of regionalisation in Europe, we launched the idea of a European Charter of Regional Self-Government. After several years of work in cooperation with regionalisation experts, we presented an initial draft European Charter of Regional Self-Government at the last plenary session of the Congress in July 1996 and requested the opinion of the Parliamentary Assembly of the Council of Europe and other bodies representing the regions.

We wish to frame a text which could become a convention open for signature by the states. The text, which includes aspects on the subsidiarity principle, should result in a Charter which would be broadly acceptable in the Council of Europe member states, despite the diversity of their regions.

The draft Charter does not give a definition of a region, but merely defines the basis of regional self-government and the fields of regional competence, without listing these in detail. The member states will be able to determine the regions to which the Charter will apply and disregard a number of articles according to their regional structures.

Finally, in line with the spirit of the conference, a special provision is devoted to states that wish to embark on a regionalisation process, in the hope that this could apply in particular to certain central and eastern European countries.

The Charter would be an important legal instrument furthering the regionalisation process and a significant contribution to the promotion of the Council of Europe's key principles - pluralist democracy, human rights, the rule of law and the sharing of power.

We hope to be able to adopt the Charter in its final form at the next plenary session of the Congress in June 1997.

This conference in Cividale has provided an opportunity to pool experiences of regional organisation. I would like to remind you that experiences are also being shared on a daily basis in a very practical way, thanks to a Congress initiative which I regard as highly significant and valuable: the local democracy embassies.

These embassies, which are small but have a high level of commitment, help encourage and support local initiatives with a view to promoting coexistence between the various communities in Croatia, the Federal Republic of Yugoslavia, Slovenia, Bosnia and Herzegovina and the former Yugoslav Republic of Macedonia.

We currently have eight local democracy embassies. They have become driving forces in local life in the host towns and bear witness to the practical action taken by towns and regions in Europe for the benefit of local authorities who wish to participate actively and fully in the process of European integration in a spirit of respect for tolerance and differences.

The role of these embassies is currently reinforced by the peace process, which must be consolidated and whose repercussions transcend the borders of the conflict areas proper. The action taken by the local democracy embassies brings together the different minority and majority groups of these areas, helps establish trust between people and furthers the process of stabilisation throughout the region.

This innovative and ambitious programme gives European municipalities, towns and regions the opportunity to establish partnerships with municipalities that wish to renew or maintain dialogue between communities. The local democracy embassies have a privileged relationship with local and regional authorities on the ground and serve as operational work bases and platforms for international cooperation.

The cooperation that has been established, for example, between the canton of Geneva and Bihac in the Una-Sana canton and my visits to Sarajevo have shown me the value of conducting specific exchange activities on site in cooperation with local authorities, but have also enabled me to gauge the difficulties which remain to be overcome. The culture of respect for others and for the standards and traditions which allow each cultural community to live, prosper and coexist is far from being a reality throughout Europe. Where there is a will to achieve it, however, there is always a way - with the help of experienced consultants where appropriate.

The Congress and the Council of Europe in general are ready to help all countries that wish to resolve these issues according to the principles of democracy, decentralisation and respect for human rights. The work done at this conference has heightened awareness and clarified the Congress's role in this difficult and sensitive field.

The achievements of these three days here in Cividale will certainly bear fruit. The proceedings of the conference and especially the final declaration will be presented in the form of a recommendation at the next plenary session of the Congress of Local and Regional Authorities of Europe.

Finally, I wish to thank the authorities of the Friuli-Venezia-Giulia Region for their warm hospitality and welcome, for overcoming all the unexpected difficulties (both practical and political) and for having brought so many delegates to this conference.

Thank you, Ladies and Gentlemen, for your participation and attention.

Prof. Claudio MAGRIS,
University of Trieste (Italy)

Small countries and large world - the river Arno and the sea

(Written contribution)

My dear friends,

I am very sorry that influenza and a high temperature have prevented me from joining you. I would of course have preferred to speak to you rather than just sending you these brief comments, which I must stress do not constitute a proper written text but are rather a series of notes dictated at the last minute on the basis of an outline of the short report which I was to have presented today.

I would have liked to speak to you of what I might call the "minority complex". A famous passage from Manzoni states that bullies and villains are responsible not only for the harm they do their victims but also for the harm which these victims go on to do to others. For instance, to expand on Manzoni, victims might respond to the hatred with which they have been persecuted by storing up hatred in their hearts, or to the violence which they have endured by acting violently towards others, etc.

Throughout history majorities (which are usually, but not always, national, since the relationship between majority and minority involves many other considerations besides ethnic ones) have often oppressed and subjugated minorities. Many minorities have not even been able to make heard their protests at the wrongs they have endured. The history of the world provides us with a myriad examples of this phenomenon. I have always been attracted by minorities and considered that we must all do our utmost to protect and defend them and publicise their existence; to me, writing, the writer's endeavours, can perhaps also be a voyage in search of forgotten minorities, an attempt to uncover their obliterated traces and wrest them from oblivion. My work entitled "Danubio" is also a journey, a quest of this kind: the traveller wends his way down the river, endeavouring to fight against its waters, the flow of time which levels and eradicates, and seeking to recover as much evidence as possible, the forgotten remains half-buried along the banks of the Danube, the vestiges of minor or major cultures, traditions and civilisations abandoned on the fringes of history and historical memory, whole peoples engulfed in the silence of forgetfulness. Leaving the Danube, I have also explored the world of the Sorbs and the tiny area occupied by the Čiči, not far from where we are now. And so we need not dwell on the many wrongs inflicted by majorities and the need for compensation, including legal damages, together with all the requisite measures for protecting minorities.

However, while minorities must begin by freeing themselves from majority oppression, they often have to break free from themselves, as well, from their own "minority complex", in order to avoid the trap described by Manzoni and cease to be the victims of wrongs which belong to the past. It is inevitable and understandable that minorities tend to be obsessed with themselves and their identity, even if such a fixation is no longer necessary. A great Polish writer who won the Nobel Prize and who was also one of the first to denounce totalitarianism in eastern Europe (though he was largely ignored

131

at the time), the poet Milosz, wrote an inspired passage describing the painful moment when, because of the prevailing national tensions, he and his family were more or less compelled to choose between the Polish and Lithuanian components of their tradition.

Because of the clash between Poles and Lithuanians, people found it very difficult, or indeed impossible, to identify with both traditions and feel that they were their heirs, albeit to differing extents. However, the poet experienced this choice not as the discovery of his true identity but as a loss, a mutilation. He recalls how one of his uncles, who was also a talented writer, told him to remember that when his nationality and identity were under threat he had to defend them most vigorously, but woe betide him if allowed this defence mechanism to absorb him completely, to become his main concern, an obsession, an idol making him forfeit all else besides.

I think this is a lesson which we all must learn. People who have a sense of belonging to a minority or who as such have been subjected to persecution or at least discrimination, tend to let this feeling take them over completely. Even if this self-defence mechanism was originally justified, it intensifies to the point of becoming an obsession, robbing those concerned of their world and finally of themselves. Kafka once wrote, with a hint of irony, that a small people cannot have a great literature. This statement is untrue, as Kafka was in fact well aware, because he was referring to Yiddish literature, which has produced excellent writers and which Kafka loved very much. In writing this sentence he knew very well that Yiddish literature was not at all the production of a small people, but rather that of a nation of great importance in both material and cultural terms. However, Kafka was referring to communities which, precisely because they were destitute, oppressed and rejected by the world around them, were liable to react by turning in on themselves and developing an all-consuming preoccupation with their identity, thus turning it into an asphyxiating spiritual endogamy, the death of the soul.

Although all members of minorities are duty-bound to combat oppression, they must also push the latter out of their minds as soon as this combat becomes redundant; they must realise that before belonging to their people, whatever its dimensions, they belong to the whole of humanity. Individuality and particularism, whether at national or any other level, are values to be defended, but only if they are taken as the basis for embracing the whole of humanity and therefore for opening up to others, to the diversity of other peoples. If identity is equated with snarling narrow-mindedness, it becomes the most backward-looking of prisons.

The fairest and freest way of experiencing one's identity is to preserve its spontaneity, without idolising or ideologising it. I am an Italian from Trieste, my father was from Friuli, I bear all these aspects in my person and I love them, but I bear them spontaneously with and within myself without ideologising them; they are an integral part of my person, but heaven forbid that they should ever become excessive and concentrate my attention on myself and my identity, so that the latter comes to determine how I regard, encounter and interact with others. When someone falls in love, the important thing is the other person, the person who is loved; when we are in love we forget ourselves, which is the only way of genuinely affirming our personality and humanity.

When identity is elevated to the status of an absolute value, it becomes an idol, and like all idols it demands blood sacrifices, as we can see from the many dreadful examples far and near. There is no such thing as a pure, unadulterated identity; we are all, thank goodness, children of Eve, that great, very "un-fussy" mother of mankind, and the quest for supposed ethnic or national purity produces a continuous destructive and self-destructive amputation of parts of ourselves, constant self-mutilation. Milosz was certainly unhappy when he had to choose between his Polish and Lithuanian sides. But people who overemphasise their identities are suspect: they show a kind of insecurity which might suggest that their feeling of identity is not at all as solid, strong and genuine as they would have us believe, in the same way as too much boasting about erotic exploits raises legitimate doubts as to the boaster's actual sexual prowess.

Genuine filial love for one's mother necessitates cutting the umbilical cord, otherwise one is doomed to extreme oedipal regression, hampering spiritual freedom and true love. Writers who love their country have also been able to speak ill of it, as Joyce did about Ireland and many great Czech writers about Prague, under the influence of their love-hate relationship with their splendid native city. We must be able to face the fact that our place is sometimes not where we thought but across a border. There is a very beautiful story which puts what I am trying to say in a nutshell, a memoir written by Biagio Marin. Fifty years on the old poet remembers being in Vienna in March 1915, before Italy had entered the first world war; he had been a university student and a passionate Italian irredentist. Having been called up before the vice-chancellor of Vienna University following a brawl between students of various different nationalities, Marin recalls telling the vice-chancellor, with all the impetuous arrogance of youth, that the Italians ("we Italians", as he put it) would have destroyed Austria. However, Marin goes on to recount how a few weeks later, after the war had spread to Italy, he had enlisted as a volunteer in the Italian army. One day, during military exercises a captain was extremely rude to him, whereupon he replied, "Captain, you are a scoundrel, we Austrians are accustomed to more class".

This ability to live on either side of a border, to know that every one of us may at some stage find himself "on the other side", constitutes genuine loyalty to one's own identity. Only those who can transcend the bare facts of their own origins can legitimately claim to love those origins; Alfieri said that the real Piedmontese were those who had been able to "de-Piedmontise" themselves. This does not mean loving one's homeland and identity less, but in fact loving them more, and more freely, just as a son who leaves home to establish a family of his own is not betraying his parents and his original family but is in fact being more loyal than those who remain childish and cannot bring themselves to leave. There is a latent danger of regression in every individual, a risk of obsessive introversion; members of minorities are perhaps more exposed to this risk, through no fault of their own: it is a result of the wrongs inflicted on them by the majority. However, they should not let this suffocate them: they should know that everyone everywhere can at some stage find himself in a minority position, and human dignity consists in being able to preserve one's freedom in such a situation. Only those who are capable of such freedom of love are entitled to speak of their fatherland, their identity, their nationality, their ethnic group or their home.

Dante said that he had conceived a great love for the city of Florence by drinking the water of the river Arno, but that our homeland is the world, just as fish are at home in every sea. We need both these waters, the extensive waters of the world and the river water of home. Without the water of the native river our love for the open seas will remain abstract and general; without the seas the native river will become a blocked stream. A unit, even a national unit, surpasses itself by coming together with greater units, not by splitting up into smaller ones. The spirit of the great harmonious unit - which is the only place where individual identities can find their station, as in the orderly, unitary diversity of a heart - is the very opposite of any rancorous separatist spirit. The river flows down to the sea and must be able to flow with it, while continuing to cherish the riverbanks along which it played as a child.

Dr Alessandra GUERRA
Councillor for Education, Culture, Community Affairs and External Relations of the Autonomous Region Friuli-Venezia-Giulia

Closing Address

Thank you. It is clearly my task to say a few words on behalf of the Regional Government following on Magris' fascinating message and above all the suggestion it contained. This, I have to say, is quite a challenge.

I shall start with two things which struck me and which are contained in the Magris' speech. He draws attention to the concept by which identity is intended as a ring fence, which is the most regressive of prisons. Then he refers more and more to the great ocean, universality and thus to that concept of something much broader which encompasses all the various microcosms which make up the complex mosaic of Europe. I believe that in this we can sum up, perhaps more from a philosophical than a practical standpoint, the dominant theme not only of today's gathering, but the whole commitment breaking out across Europe to promote minority cultures and languages.

In this regard, I would like to thank the other two hundred delegates who came from every district of Europe and I would especially like to thank them not only for participating but for the high level of contributions made here today, in that little patch of earth called Friuli-Venezia-Giulia, which in turn represents a small mosaic in the greater mosaic of Europe. I would also like to thank you because you have shown how that danger of failing memory, as Magris puts it, which is feared perhaps by all those who work to protect minority languages and cultures, is certainly overcome by those who work, because we have heard tell of the great ocean as a reference to us all, thus to Europe. We have heard tell not of closing inwards but of opening outwards and above all we have heard the voice of a European consciousness which perhaps we, who administer, do not realize we have, but which is slowly stealing into every corner of Europe. I believe that this message and this common sentiment is extremely important and it is the message which every one of us, in our work and the dress which at certain times in our lives we wear, must continue to bear.

Having said this, I would like to go on simply and very briefly to a series of somewhat technical reflections which have emerged from these three days and which can summarize the commitments already amply discussed in turn by the speakers and chairmen in these three days, who I thank. These are commitments which particularly concern this region, but also I believe all the regions of Europe, which can above all be described as a commitment by every single European land and region to ensure that its own State ratifies the Charter for Regional and Minority Languages. I believe that this is the first thing we must be asked to do, as the Friuli-Venezia-Giulia region, because as you know the Italian State has not yet done so. Then I think it is important for all the Regions of Europe to commit themselves so that their States sign and above all accept fully all the texts on minority human rights, and regional and minority languages. There are so many of them, and it seems to me to run like a thread through this conference that few of them enjoy the attention of states at international level.

Lastly, that all the regions, in their relations with their own State, should endeavour to ensure that some rights sacrosanct to minorities are protected, first through practical measures, then through legislation which enshrines those rights, in particular so that the Regions can take direct responsibility for schools and education, fundamental if the seeds of minorities are not to be lost and diluted as has so often happened before, as recalled by Magris in the last report, in many European lands. Then they must strive to strengthen and consolidate relations between regions which contain various minorities, respecting the international policies of States with neighbouring regions, which have similar languages, customs and culture. And, finally, they must endeavour to ensure that regional legislation becomes ever closer to the people, so as to safeguard the speech and culture of people in their land of origin. In this connection, as I said at the beginning, our aim is not so much to protect and safeguard Slovenian and Friulian language and culture, but to reach a point where we promote laws which extend safeguards, protection and promotion of all minorities present in this region. We do not want, so perhaps it has been one of the slightly controversial points, to hold ourselves up as a model region, indeed, we have so much to learn from other regions of Europe and we are very indebted in that respect.

So we hope, as I also said at the beginning, that when we read again calmly and in security, as I believe we will, all the documents which this meeting and these three days have produced, our regions will have important ideas to enable them to legislate and legislate in increasingly European and less and less inward-looking terms.

So, I thank you once again for the opportunity to be your host, and I thank the speakers and participants, hoping more than ever that our regional borders will be open and that these changes will affect not just our region but all of Europe, making our region part of your home.

Thank you again.

III. FINAL DECLARATION

———

1.   The participants in the Conference on Federalism, Regionalism, Local Autonomy and Minorities, held by the Congress of Local and Regional Authorities of the Council of Europe (CLRAE) and the Friuli-Venezia-Giulia Autonomous Region in Cividale del Friuli (Italy) from 24 to 26 October 1996:

2.   Wish to thank Friuli-Venezia-Giulia Autonomous Region most sincerely for its kind hospitality and the excellent organisation of the Conference;

3.   Considering the texts of the United Nations, the OSCE, the Central European Initiative and the European Parliament concerning minorities;

4.   Considering that the problem of linguistic and ethnic minorities, while demanding national action, has now become a problem of democracy and respect for human rights which therefore concerns Europe as a whole and thus warrants international regulation;

5.   Considering that the CLRAE, in Resolution 232 (1992), called for this conference to be organised to consider examples of the involvement of minorities in local self-government in Europe with a view to drawing up appropriate recommendations;

6.   Considering that, from the internal point of view of States, the legal forms of federalism, regionalism and local self-government actually merely amount to differing methods of applying the principle of subsidiarity, which the European Charter of Local Self-Government defines as meaning that "public responsibilities shall generally be exercised, in preference, by those authorities which are closest to the citizen. Allocation of responsibility to another authority should weigh up the extent and nature of the task and requirements of efficiency and economy";

7.   Considering that neither international law in general nor the treaties dealing with the problem of minorities, in particular the two instruments adopted by the Council of Europe (the European Charter for Regional or Minority Languages and the Framework Convention for the Protection of National Minorities), guarantee minorities a genuine and universally recognised right to manage their own affairs in the areas where they live, even though Article 7.1 (b) of the Charter requires the Contracting Parties to respect the geographical area of each regional or minority language in order to ensure that existing or new administrative divisions do not constitute an obstacle to the promotion of such languages;

8.   Considering, however, that certain bilateral treaties and many national constitutions do provide for some degree of local or regional self-government by minorities;

9.   Considering also that Parliamentary Assembly Recommendation 1201 (1993) states that, in regions where they are in a majority, persons belonging to a national minority should have the right to have at their disposal appropriate local or autonomous authorities or to have a special status, matching the specific historical and territorial situation and in accordance with the domestic legislation of the State;

10.   Having considered examples of local or regional self-government enjoyed by minorities in Finland, Italy, Spain and certain central and east European countries;

11.   Considering that, in accordance with the principles of the European Charter of Local Self-Government, self-government can be defined here as the right and the ability of local and regional authorities, within the limits of the law, to regulate and manage a substantial share of public affairs under their own responsibility and in the interests of the local population;

12.   Whereas local and regional authorities can be focal points for debating and solving problems of minorities, coexistence, solidarity and mutual acceptance;

13.   While recognising that ethnic criteria should not be the only grounds on which particular areas should be granted some degree of local or regional self-government, and that historical or cultural traditions and geographical or economic situations may also warrant the granting of special powers or responsibilities to autonomous authorities;

14.   Believe, nevertheless, that under certain circumstances, for instance when there are high concentrations of persons belonging to a minority on the territory of a municipality, province or region, when certain historical traditions exist or when particular areas are culturally and linguistically homogenous, etc, local self-government within the geographical area concerned is a very effective means of helping to solve the problem of minorities while avoiding the development of separatist tendencies;

15.   Considering that citizens' loyalty to the State is based on the respect of human rights and the principles of democracy;

16.   Believe also that, in some cases, cultural autonomy, which is a crucial element of local or regional self-government by minorities in their own areas, may, under certain circumstances, be an alternative to such self-government or may add to it;

17.   Declare that minorities' territorial self-government should not be limited to States having federal or regional structures, but is also possible and desirable in unitary States; moreover, it does not endanger the State's sovereignty and territorial integrity;

18.   Stress the fact that the self-government enjoyed by minorities does not necessarily have to take the same form as that granted to local or regional authorities, but may - and, indeed, must - include more extensive responsibilities, particularly with regard to culture and language, which should be backed up by the necessary funding;

19.   Recall that transfrontier cooperation can contribute to the peaceful settlement of national minority issues as emphasized in the declaration of heads of State and government adopted in Vienna on 18 October 1993;

20.   Stress that national measures guaranteeing effective equality among all State citizens and the appropriate legislative protection of minorities are, in any case, a pre-requisite to minorities' territorial autonomy;

A.   Recommend that the CLRAE draw up a draft recommendation to governments indicating:

a.   under what circumstances - for instance, ethnically homogenous areas, strong sense of belonging to a minority community, linguistic and cultural traditions that differ from those of the majority population, or the presence of different minority groups, etc - the relevant minorities should have the right to an appropriate form of self-government (municipal, provincial, regional), it being ensured that they continue fully to respect the territorial integrity of the state concerned and remain loyal to it;

b.   the powers which the autonomous authorities concerned should, as a rule, be granted, as well as the right of such authorities to cooperate and form consortia in conformity with article 10 of the European Charter of Local Self-Government;

c.   the means for ensuring that minorities' local and regional self-government actually help to integrate them into their national communities and European society as a whole, rather than isolating them from the latter;

d.   the criteria to be applied when defining the geographic limits of the autonomous authorities, where the concentration of the minority population justifies the establishment of such authorities;

e.   the need to consult, if appropriate through their representative organisations, the members of the minorities concerned, with regard to the granting, extension or any other modification of minority self-government at local or regional level in order to reach a consensus among all those concerned;

f.   the forms local self-government should take and the institutions it should involve, as well as the way they should operate, when geographical, economic, social or historical factors mean that the territory of the authority concerned is populated by groups from different ethnic, religious, linguistic and cultural backgrounds;

g.   ways and means of promoting transfrontier cooperation between local and regional authorities in whose territory a significant number of minority members is concentrated;

B.   Also recommend that the CLRAE take account of this declaration when finalising the draft European Charter of Regional Self-Government.

IV. LIST OF PARTICIPANTS

———

AUTRICHE/AUSTRIA

M. Karl ANDERWALD
Amt der Kärtner Landesregierung
Arnulfplatz 1
9020 KLAGENFURT

M. Klaus FABJAN
Minister
Federal Ministry for Foreign Affairs
Ballhausplatz 1
1014 VIENNA

Mme Cornelia KOGOJ
Lerchengasse 15/25
1080 WIEN

M. Emmerich KOROSCH
Amt der Kärntner Landesregierung
Arnulfplatz 1
A - 9020 KLAGENFURT

M. Hans MUSKOVICH
Land Burgenland
Freiheisplatz 1
A - 7000 EISENSTADT

M. Fortunat OLIP
Narodni svet koroshik Slovencev
Rat der Kärntner Slowenen
10 Oktoberstr. 25/IV
9020 KLAGENFURT

Mme Mirjam POLZER-SRIENZ
Feistritz 39
9149 ST. MICHAEL

BELGIQUE/BELGIUM

Mme Andrée GUILLAUME-
VANDERROOST
Députée bruxelloise
Conseil de la Région de Bruxelles-Capitale
Avenue de l'Astronomie 21
1210 BRUXELLES

M. Nicolas LEVRAT
Université Libre de Bruxelles
50 bld. F.D. Roosevelt - CP. 137
B - BRUXELLES

Mme Marie NAGY
Députée bruxelloise
Conseil de la Région de Bruxelles-Capitale
Avenue de l'Astronomie 21
1210 BRUXELLES

M. Louis ROPPE
Président
Union des Villes et Communes belges a.s.b.l.
53 rue d'Arlon
1040 BRUXELLES

Mme Andrea-Maria SEELING-KRAINER

Land Burgenland
39 rue Montoyer
B - 1000 BRUXELLES

M. Vincent VAGMAN

Attaché de Cabinet de M. Cauwengerghe
Avenue Bonesse 29
B - 5100 JAMBES-NAMUR

M. Guy VANHENGEL

Député bruxellois
Conseil de la Région de Bruxelles-Capitale
Avenue de l'Astronomie 21
1210 BRUXELLES

BULGARIE/BULGARIA

Mme Maria STOYANOVA

City Counsellor
Sofia Municipality
Tsar Boris III 124
1612 SOFIA

CROATIE/CROATIA

Mme Mirjana DOMINI

Head of the Institute for Migration
and Nationalities
Trg Stjepana Radica 3
10 000 ZAGREB

M. Darko GÖTTLICHER

Counsellor of Deputy Prime Minister
Government of the Republic of Croatia
Trg. Su. Marka 2
10 000 ZAGREB

M. Ivan IAKOVCIC

Regione Istria

Mme Jasmina KOVACEVIC-CAVLOVIC

Head of Department
Croatian Minorities and Expatriates
Ministry of Foreign Affairs
Trg. N.S. Zrinskog 7-8
10 000 ZAGREB

M. Stanko NICK

Ambassador, Chief Legal Adviser
Ministry of Foreign Affairs
Trg. Zrinskog 8
10 000 ZAGREB

Mme Vesna PICHLER

Verein der Deutschen-Österreicher
Kroatien
Zentrale - Osijek
Europske Avenije 8, P.F. 222
31 000 OSIJEK

Mme Lorena SVERKO

Consulente Collaborazione Inter.
Regione Istria
Via Maestra s.n.
524714 VERTEMEGLIO

RÉPUBLIQUE TCHÈQUE/
CZECH REPUBLIC

M. Daniel KORTE

Government of the Czech Republic
Nabrezi Eduarda Benese 4
CZ - 118 01 PRAGUE 1

M. Petr VANEK

Local Authorities
City of Ostrava
Prokesovo namesti 8
729 30 OSTRAVA

DANEMARK/DENMARK

M. Pär STENBÄCK

Secretary General
Nordic Council of Ministers
Storastrandstraede 18
1255 COPENHAGEN

ESTONIE/ESTONIA

M. Mart NUTT

Estonian Parliament
Lossi Plats 1A
EE - 0100 TALLINN

M. Tonis SEESMAA

Estonian Parliament
Lossi Plats 1A
EE - 0100 TALLINN

M. Juhan SILLASTE

Executive Director
Association of Estonian Cities
12 Vana-Viru Str.
EE 0001 TALLINN

REPUBLIQUE FEDERALE DE YOUGOSLAVIE/
FEDERAL REPUBLIC OF YUGOSLAVIA

M. Omeragic BAJRAM

Region - Sanjak - Novi Pazar
Tel/fax: (381) 20 20 083
Sanjak Information Centre - Geneva
K.H.U.R.B.
1211.2 Depot
GENEVE

144

FINLANDE/FINLAND

Ms Susanne BJORKHOLM

LLB, Executive Secretary AAlands
Landshapsstyrelse
PB 60
22101 MARIEHAMN (Aaland)

Ms Kristina WIKBERG

Head of the Swedish-Speaking Secretariat
The Association of Finnish Local Authorities
Toinen Linja 14
00530 HELSINKI

Ms Ulrika WOLF-KNUTS

ABO Akademi University
Religionsvetenskap & Folkloristik
20500 ABO

FRANCE

M. Georges DE RIVAS

Secrétariat Général
FORUM
7 rue de la Vega
75012 PARIS

Mme Laura DE ROSE

Responsable de Commission
Assemblée des Régions d'Europe
20 Place des Halles
67054 STRASBOURG

M. Paul STAES

Membre de l'Assemblée Parlementaire
du Conseil de l'Europe
STRASBOURG

M. Jean-Marie WOEHRLING

Président du Tribunal Administratif
de Strasbourg
31 Avenue de la Paix - BP 1038
67070 STRASBOURG

ALLEMAGNE/GERMANY

Mr Karl AHRENS

Präsident
AGEG - Arbeitsgemeinschaft Europäischer
Grenzregionen
Euscheder Str. 362
48599 GRONAU

M. Ludwig ELLE

Federal Union of European Nationalities
Sorbian Institut
Bahnhofstrasse 6
02625 BAUTZEN

M. Jens GABBE

Generalsekretar
AGEG - Arbeitsgemeinschaft Europäischer
Grenzregionen
Euscheder Str. 362
48599 GRONAU

M. Peter RABE

Vice-President of the CLRAE
Government of Lower Saxony
Hinrich-Wilhelm-Kopf-Platz 1
30159 HANNOVER

HONGRIE/HUNGARY

M. Jenö BÖSZÖRMÉNYI

Staff Member, Department for Political
Analysis
Government Office for Hungarian
Minorities Abroad
4 Kossuth L. Ter
1055 BUDAPEST

M. Laszlo DOMITER

Fuzesi Str. 15
9970 SZENTGOTTHARD

Mme Gyula ERDÖDY

Member of the County Council
General Assembly of County Council
Rákóczi str. 11
7623 PECS

M. István HAJDU

Councellor of Minorities
Bacs-Kiskun County General Assembly
Deák F., tér 3
6000 KECSKEMET

M. Gabor KLENCSAR

Secretary
Minorities Working Group Alpe-Adria
Csokonai 3
7400 KAPOSVAR

M. Peter KOVACS

Université de Miskolc
Perczel u. 43/b
3529 MISKOLC

M. Jozsef OSZTROGONACS

President of Croatian Association
Bacs-Kiskun County
Deák F., tér 3
6000 KECSKEMET

M. Matyas SCHMATOVICH

Participian
ALPE ADRIA Workcommunity
Arpad u. 32
4022 GYÓRG

M. László SZÁSZFALVI

President
Minorities Working Group Alpe-Adria
Csokonai 3
7400 KAPOSVAR

Mme Madgolna TAMAS

European Projects Officer
Bacs-Kiskun County General Assembly
Deák F., tér 3
6000 KECSKEMET

ITALIE/ITALY

M. Eugenio AMBROSI

Funzionario Servizio Rapporti Esterni
Regione Autonoma Friuli-Venezia-Giulia
Via San Francesco 37
34100 TRIESTE

M. Stefano BITTI

Consigliere e Vice Presidente Consiglio
Provincia di Roma
Via IV November 119/A
00187 ROMA

M. Stefan BÖCKLER

Associazione Italo-Tedesca di Sociologia
Via Verdi 26
38100 TRENTO

M. Antonio BORGHESI

Presidente
Provincia di Verona
Via Santa Maria Antica 1
37100 VERONA

M. Martin Luis BRECELJ

Segretario
Slovenska Skupnost -Unione Slovena
Via G. Gallina 5/111
34122 TRIESTE

M. Stefano BUKOVEC

Dottore in sc. politiche
SSK - US - Partito dell'Union Slovena
Via Foscolo 24
34170 GORIZIA

M. Giulio BUFFO

Consigliere
Provincia di Roma
Via IV Novembre 119/A
00187 ROMA

M. Giovanni CASTELLANETA

Cap Servizio - Coordinamento Regionale
Ministero Affari Esteri
P. le Farnesina
00100 ROMA

147

M. Sergio CECOTTI

Presidente
Regione Autonoma Friuli-Venezia-Giulia
Piazza Unità d'Italia 1
TRIESTE

M. Guglielmo CERNO

Unione degli Sloveni
della Provincia di Udine
Via 4 Agosto 8
33043 CIVIDALE DEL FRIULI

M. Luigi COLOMBIN

Dirigente Regionale
Regione Lazio
Via Caravaggio 99
00100 ROMA

M. Giancarlo CRUDER

Presidente
Consiglio Regionale
Regione Autonoma Friuli-Venezia-Giulia
Piazza Oberdan 6
TRIESTE

M. Piero DI MAGGIO

Dirigente Superiore
Presidenza Regione Siciliana
"Palazzo d'Orleans"
Piazza Indipendenza
90100 PALERMO

M. Roberto DI GIOVAN PAOLO

Segretario Generale Aggiunto
AICCRE
Piazza di Trevi 86
00187 ROMA

M. Giorgio DOMINESE

Centro Studi Nord Est
San Marco 3226/8
30124 VENEZIA

M. Pierino DONADA

Segretario
AICCRE
Federazione Regionale Friuli-Venezia-Giulia
Piazza XX Settembre 2
33100 UDINE

Mme Gina FASAN

Sindaco
Comune di Sacile
Piazza del Popolo
33077 SACILE

Mme Maria FERLETIC

Magistrale
Confederazione delle org. slovache
34170 GORIZIA

M. Alberto FONZO

Laurea
Regione Friuli-Venezia-Giulia
Via Dormisch 65/5
33100 UDINE

M. Giovanni FRAU

Prof. ordinario nell'Università
Università degli studi di Udine
(privato: via Marghera 30
33100 UDINE)

M. Guido GERIN

Presidente
Istituto Internazionale
Studi Diritti dell'Uomo
Via Cantù 10
34127 TRIESTE

Mme Alessandra GUERRA

Assessore Regionale
Affari Comunitari e Rapporti Esterni
Regione Autonoma Friuli-Venezia-Giulia
Via San Francesco 37
TRIESTE

M. Riccardo ILLY

Sindaco
Comune di Trieste
Piazza Unità d'Italia 4
TRIESTE

Mme Adriana JANEZIC

Dottore in sociologia
Regione Autonoma Friuli-Venezia-Giulia
Direttore del Servizio lingue regionalie
minoritarie
Via San Francesco 37
34100 TRIESTE

M. Klaus LUTHER

Provincia Autonoma di Bolzano
Palazzo Provinciale
39100 BOLZANO

M. Claudio MAGRIS

Università degli Studi di Trieste
P.le Europa 1
TRIESTE

M. Gianfranco MARTINI

Membro del Congresso dei Poteri Locali
e Regionali
AICCRE
Piazza di Trevi 86
00187 ROMA

Mme Danila MOLL

Assessore ai Servizi Sociali e Cultuarali
Provincia di Pavia
Piazza Italia 2
27100 PAVIA

M. Aldo MOLTIFIORI

Responsabile Settore Enti Locali
Lega Nord
Via Bellerio 41
20161 MILANO

M. Faustino NAZZI

Insegnante
ITA
Via Premariacco 13/1
CIVIDALE

M. Luigi NONNI

Consigliere
Provincia di Roma
Via IV Novembre 119/A
00187 ROMA

M. Lucio PERESSI

Società Filologia Friulana
Via Manin 18
33100 UDINE

M. Ugo POLI

AICCRE
Ass. Italiana per il Consiglio dei Comuni
d'Europa
Via per Basovizza 25/14
34016 TRIESTE

M. Gilberto PRESSACCO

Conservatorio "Tomadini"
UDINE

M. Ludovico Nevio PUNTIN

AICCRE
Ass. Italiana per il Cons. dei Comuni
d'Europa
Via per Basovizza 25/14
34016 TRIESTE

M. Marino QUALIZZA

Direttore
Scuola Diocesana di Form. Socio-Politica
Saint-Siège - Seminario Arcivescovile
Viale Ungheria 18
33100 UDINE

M. Emil Petru RATIU

Asociatia Culturale LU
Istro-Rumeni "Andrei Glavina"
Via delle Fornaci 24
00165 ROMA

Mme Melita RICHTER-MALABOTTA

Croatian Sociological Association
Via Franca 2
34123 TRIESTE

M. Riccardo RUTTAR

Istituo Sloveno Ricerche SLORI
Borgo San Domenico 50
33043 CIVIDALE DEL FRIULI

M. Diego SANTORO

Pubblicista
CAPHR
Via XXV Aprile 6
34077 RONCHI DEI LEGIONARI

Mme Silvia SANZINI

Redattrice
Rivista "Filodiretto" - Lega Nord
Via Bellerio 41
20161 MILANO

M. Silvana SCHIAVI FACCHIN

Docente di Didattica della Lingue Moderne
Dipartimento di Scienze Filosofiche
Università di Udine
Via Antonini 8
33100 UDINE

M. E. SNIDERSIG

Assessore alla Cultura di Cividale
COMUNE DI CIVIDALE

Mme Paola TABOR

Funzionario Servizio Rapporti Esterni
Regione Autonoma Friuli-Venezia-Giulia
Via San Francesco 37
34100 TRIESTE

M. Mario TOROS

Ente Friuli nel Mondo

M. Dusan UDOVIC

Slovenska Kulturno Gospodarska Zveza
Unione Culturale Economica Slovena
Via San Francesco 20/111
34133 TRIESTE

M. Marino VOCCI

Circolo di cultura istro-veneto "Istria"
e "Promoistria" srl - D.o.o.
Via dei Fiordalisi 10/5
34016 TRIESTE

M. Hans ZELGER

Presidente
Consorzio dei Comuni - Bolzano
Lungo Talvera S. Quirino 10
39100 BOLZANO

LETTONIE/LATVIA

M. Visvaldis RADELIS

Chairman
Council of Talsi City
7 Kareiv 34 Str.
LV - 3200 TALSI

Mme Lilia SAVICHA

Senior Adviser of Dep. of National Affairs
Ministry of Justice
Brivibas bd 36
LV - 1536 RIGA

LITUANIE/LITHUANIA

M. Gintaras MORKIS

Member of CLRAE
Council of Plunge District
Str. Pramonés 45
LT - 5640 PLUNGE

M. Juozapas PALIAKAS

Counsellor, Vice Governor of County
Kaipeda Regional Council
Danes Str. 17
LT - 5800 KAIPEDA

M. Klemensas RIMSELIS

Counsellor, Char. of City Development
and Self-Government
Kaunas Municipality
Laisvès Al. 96
3000 KAUNAS

M. Severinas VAITIEKUS

Deputy Director
Department of Regional Problems and
National Minorities of the Government of
Lithuania
30 Kostiuskos Str.
2600 VILNIUS

LUXEMBOURG

M. Christian GLÖCHNER

Institut Régional Intracommunautaire
a.s.b.l.
BP 1704 - 1, ave. de la Gare
1017 LUXEMBOURG

PAYS-BAS/NETHERLANDS

M. Jonathon COHEN

Foundation of Inter-Ethnic Relations
2500 THE HAGUE

M. Tonnis RICHT DOESBURG

Provincie Gelderland
Postbus 9090
NL - 6800 GX ARNHEM

POLOGNE/POLAND

Mme Maria GROBELNA-CHELMINSKA

Conseiller du Ministre
Office du Conseil des Ministres
ul. Litewska 2/4
PL - 00583 VARSOVIE

M. Leon KIERES

President
Regional Assembly of Wrockaw Voivodeship
Pl. Powstancow Warszawy 1
50951 WROCLAW

M. Alexander MASLEJ

Zjednoczenie Lemkov
Ul. Broniewkiego 9/7
38-300 GORLICE

M; Kowalskyj MYCHAJTO

Vereinigung der Lanken
ul. Armii Ludowej 16/5
66-400 GORZOWK KILKO

M. Waclaw SZLANTA

Zjednoczenie Lemkow
Ul. Hallera 20/19
38-300 GORLICE

ROUMANIE/ROMANIA

M. Vasile ALDROFAN

Vice-Président
Conseil Départemental Bistrita-Nasaud
Piata Petru Rares 1
4400 BISTRITA

M. Lucian ATANASIU

Director
Arad County Council
B-Dul Revolutiei 75
2900 ARAD

M. Gheorge BARBU	President of the County Council Hunedoara County Council 1 December Street 35 2700 DEVA
M. Pamfil BERCEAN	Vice-Président Consiliul Judetean Maramures Baia Mare Jud. Maramures Str. Gh. Sincai 46 4800 BAIA MARE
M. Ioan BOLDOR	Consilier Consiliul Judetean Maramures Baia Mare Jud. Maramures Str. Gh. Sincai 46 4800 BAIA MARE
M. Alic CIPRIAN	Head of Foreign Relations Hunedoara County Council 1 December Street 35 2700 DEVA
M. Ivan DAN	President of Arad Region Arad County Council B-Dul Revolutiei 75 2900 ARAD
Mme Lorena FILIMON	Referant External Relation ARAD County Council B-Dul Revolutiei 75 2900 ARAD
M. Petru-Alexandru FRATEAN	Vice-Président Conseil du Département de Mures Rue Primariei 2 4300 TIRGU MURES
Mme Jenica GRAUR	Fonctionnaire Conseil Départamental Bistrita-Nasaud Piata Petru Rares 1 4900 BISTRITA
M. Costantin IONASCU	Inspecteur Gouvernemental Le Gouvernement de Roumanie Dept. pour l'Administration Publique Locale Piata Victoriei 1 BUCAREST

M. Petru JURCAN

Diplomat
Ministry of Foreign Affairs

M. Gábor KOLUMBÁN

President
County Council Hargita-Romania
Piata Libertati 5
4100 MIERCUREA CIUC

Mme Gabriela-Liliana MARINCEA

Translator
Council of Covasna District
Piata Libertatii 4
4000 SFINTU GHEORGHE -
JUDET COVASNA

M. Arpad ORBAN

President of the Council of Covasna District
Piata Libertatii 4
4000 SFINTU GHEORGHE -
JUDET COVASNA

M. Ferencz PAL

Counsellor
Council of Covasna District
Piata Libertatii 4
4000 SFINTU GHEORGHE -
JUDET COVASNA

M. Stefan PUTURA

Conseiller Départemental
Conseil Départemental Bistrita-Nasaud
Piata Petru Rares 1
4400 BISTRITA

M. Iosif REDL

Secrétaire
Conseil Départemental Bistrita-Nasaud
Piata Petru Rares 1
4400 BISTRITA

M. Iosif SZANISZLO

Député-Maire
Conseil local
Municipal Baia Mare
Str. Gh. Sincai 37
4800 BAIA MARE

Mme Pompilia SZELLNER

Counsellor
ARAD County Council
B-Dul Revolutiei 75
2900 ARAD

M. Smarandach Calin VINTILA

Vicepresidente
Consiliul Judetean Maramures
Baia Mare Jud. Maramures
Str. N. lorga 2171
4800 BAIA MARE

M. György-Lajos VIRAG

Vice-president
Conseil du Département de Mures
Rue Primariei 2
4300 TIRGU MURES

FÉDÉRATION DE RUSSIE/
RUSSIAN FEDERATION

M. Sergey BOROZDIN

Counsellor, Expert of the Delegation
Council of the Federation
26 Bol Dmitrovka
103426 MOSCOW

M. Marjam JANDIEVA

Unione Donne del Nord del Caucaso
Inguscezia
Ulica K. Marx 16, App. 36 - Balasina
143900 MOSCOW

M. Nikolai KARTSEV

Secretary of the Delegation
Council of the Federation
26 Bd Dmitrovka
103426 MOSCOW

M. Alexander ROMANOV

Counsellor
Council of the Federation
26 Bd Dmitorvka
103426 MOSCOW

M. Vladimir SHTYGASHEV

Chairman
Parliament of the Republic of Khakassia
67 Lenin pr.
662619 ABAKAN, Rep. KHAKASSIA

M. Anatoly P. SYTCHEV

Chairman
Novosibirsk Regional Council of Deputies
3 Kirov Str.
630011 NOVOSIBIRSK

M. Stansislav V. VAVILOV

Chairman
Legislative Association of the Jewish
Autonomous
Region
18, 60 Let. USSR pr
682200 BIROBIDZHAN

SLOVAQUIE/SLOVAKIA

M. Istvan BATTA

Együttélés - Spoluzitie - Coexistance
P.O. Box 44 - Prazska 7
81499 BRATISLAVA/POZSONY/PRESSBURG

M. Jozef PROKES

National Council of the Slovak Republic
Mudronova 1
812 80 BRATISLAVA

M. Pavol SEGES

Municipal Office
Nàm M.R. Stefanika 1
955 28 TOPOLCANY

M. Richard VOLEK

Local Authorities - Mayor
Mierova 21
827 05 BRATISLAVA

SLOVÉNIE/SLOVENIA

M. Andrej COKERT

Government Service for Local Self-
Government
Trzaska 42
1000 LJUBLJANA

M. Silvo DEVETAK

ECERS, University of Maribor
Mladinska 9
SLO - 2000 MARIBOR

M. Toni GOMISCEK

Laurea in sociologia
Radio Koper
Capodistria
Studio Nova Gorica
Rejceva 6
5000 NOVA GORICA

M. Aurelio JURI

Mayor of the City of Koper
Street G. Verdi 10
6000 KOPER

Mme Sonja NOVAK-LUKANOVIC

Senior Researcher
Institute for Ethnic Studies
Erjavceva 26
1000 LJUBLJANA

M. Patrick QUINET

Delegate
Local Democracy Embassy
Partizanska 47 III
SLO - 2000 MARIBOR

M. Marjan TERPIN

Slovenska Skuporost-Unioni Slovena
Gorizia- Via III
ARMATA 179

ESPAGNE/SPAIN

M. Itziar ALBA

Délégué
Parlement Basque
Becerro de Bengoa s/n
E - 01005 VITORIA-GASTEIZ

M. Nekane ALZELAI

Délégué
Parlement Basque
Becerro de Bengoa s/n
E - 01005 VITORIA-GASTEIZ

M. Enriqueta BENITO

Délégué
Parlement Basque
Becerro de Bengoa s/n
E - 01005 VITORIA-GASTEIZ

M. Ramon CAMP I BATALLA

Député
Le Parlement de Catalogne
Parc Ciutadella s/n
08003 BARCELONA

M. José CASTRO ALVAREZ

FEMP
C/ Jardines Ramiro Sabell Mosquerra
E - 36860 PUENTEAREAS

M. Higini CLOTAS CIERCO

Député - Porte parole Groupe socialiste
Le Parlement de Catalogne
Parc Ciutadella s/n
08003 BARCELONA

M. Juan Carlos DA SILVA

Délégué
Parlement Basque
Becerro de Bengoa s/n
E - 01005 VITORIA-GASTEIZ

M. Tomas GARCIA

Délégué
Parlement Basque
Becerro de Bengoa s/n
E - 01005 VITORIA-GASTEIZ

M. Belen GREAVES

Délégué
Parlement Basque
Becerro de Bengoa s/n
E - 01005 VITORIA-GASTEIZ

M. Ignacio LATIERRO

Délégué
Parlement Basque
Becerro de Bengoa s/n
E - 01005 VITORIA-GASTEIZ

M. José Maria MUÑOA

Délégué du Président pour les Relations
extérieures
Gouvernement Basque
Navarra 2
01006 VITORIA-GASTEIZ

M. Domenec SESMILO I RIUS

Vice-Président
Le Parlement de Catalogne
Parc Ciutadella s/n
08003 BARCELONA

M. Carlos Maria URQUIJO

Délégué
Parlement Basque
Becerro de Bengoa s/n
E - 01005 VITORIA-GASTEIZ

SUISSE/SWITZERLAND

M. Romedi ARQUINT

Union fédérale de la Communauté
européenne
CH - 7526 CINUOSCHEL

M. Thomas FLEINER

Université de Fribourg
Institut du Fédéralisme
FRIBOURG

M. Claude HAEGI

Président du Congrès des Pouvoirs Locaux
et Régionaux de l'Europe/
President of the Congress of Local
and Regional Authorities of Europe
Council of Europe
67075 STRASBOURG

M. Fabrizio TASCHETTA

Adjoint scientifique
Département Fédéral des Affaires
Etrangères
3003 BERNE

"L'EX-REPUBLIQUE YOUGOSLAVE DE MACEDOINE" / "THE FORMER YUGOSLAV REPUBLIC OF MACEDONIA"

M. Plamen GEORGIEVSKI

Secretary
Association of Municipalities and Towns
Ul. Zeleznicka b.b.
P.O. Box 377
91000 SKOPJE

M. Blagoja SILJANOSKI

Mayor of Ohria
Association of Municipalities and Towns
Ul. Dimitar Vlahov
97300 OHRIA

UKRAINE

M. Aladar ADAM

Head of the Romani Jag Society
Glinka Street 43
UZHGOROD

M. Josef ADAM

Head of the Regional Roma Society in
Uzhgorod
Donskaja Street 4
UZHGOROD

M. Ernes BUCHKO

Head of Roma's Renaissance Society
Lehotskoho Str. 50/55
UZHGOROD

M. Arpad DALMAY

Head of the Hungarian Cultural Society
Hunyadi Street 7
BEREGSZASZ

M. Zoltan FABRI

Vice-President
Scientific Hungarological Society
Zankovetskoi Street 36/20
294015 UZHGOROD

Mme Svetlana HARTMANN

Editor in Chief
Newspaper "Deutscher Kanal"
6, ul. Koroleva, apt. 7
252148 KYIV

M. Peter HODJMAS

Lawyer
Zankovetskaya Street 19/71
294015 UZHGOROD

Mme Svetlana KALMYKOVA

Interpreter
Newspaper "Deutscher Kanal"
6, ul. Koroleva, apt. 7
252148 KYIV

M. Konstiantyn KOVALTCHOUK

Historian
The Christian Democratic Alliance of
Romanians
in Ukraine
Chernovtsy Region, Gliboka District
275430 Village Valea Cozmin

Mme Margarita MIHALOVA

Interpreter
Zankovetshaya Street 2/100
UZHGOROD

Mme Marta PEREVUZNIK

Representative of Greek-Cath. Association
Zaliznithna Street 44/7
UZHGOROD

M. Viktor PILIPENKO

President
Foundation of Local Self-Government
Lesi Ukrainki 26
KYIV

M. Petro POSTEVKA

Master of Arts in Education
The Christian Democratic Alliance of
Romanians
in Ukraine
Chernovtsy Region
Gliboka District
Sverdlok str. 12 A
275500 GLIBOKA

Mme Natalia SHYMANSKA

Executive Director
Association of Democratic Council of
Ukraine
98 Chernovoarmiyska
252005 KYIV

Mme Galina STOKOLESNA

Member of Russian Association in
Subcarpathia
Zankovetskaya Street 88/2
UZHGOROD

M. Ivan TALABISKA

Head of the Regional
Carpatho-Rusyns Society in Svalyva
Village Suskovo 170
SVALYAVSKI REGION

M. Ivan TURYANITSA	Head of Carpatho-Rusyns Universitetski Pereulok 6/20 294000 UZHGOROD
Mme Zirka VERECH	Head of the Catholic Oecumenical Women's Association in Uzhgorod Schevchenko Street 14 UZHGOROD
M. Eugen VERESH	Member of Scientific Hungariological Society in Subcarpathia Schevchenko Street 14 UZHGOROD
Mme Mariya YARCHICH	Secretary of Rusyn's Society Kanalno-Nasipnaya Street 10/28 UZHGOROD

SECRÉTARIAT DU CONSEIL DE L'EUROPE
SECRETARIAT OF THE COUNCIL OF EUROPE

M. Ferdinando ALBANESE	Directeur de l'Environnement et des Pouvoirs Locaux/Director of Environment and Local Authorities
M. Carlos GRAU TANNER	Administrateur du Secrétariat du Congrès/ Administrator of the Congress Secretariat
M. Giampaolo CORDIALE	Secrétariat du Congrès/Congress Secretariat
Mme Jeanne PAGOT	Assistante administrative du Secrétariat du Congrès/Administrative Assistant of the Congress Secretariat
Mme Jackie RENAUDIN-SIDDALL	Assistante du Secrétariat du Congrès/Assistant of the Congress Secretariat

Journaliste/Journalist

M. Roberto TUMBARELLO	Journaliste, Conseil de l'Europe/ Journalist, Council of Europe

Interprètes/Interpreters

Mme Liliana DAVANZO	Interprète du Conseil de l'Europe Via San L. in Selva 25 34100 TRIESTE

Mme Elisabeth JENNINGS

Interprète du Conseil de l'Europe
Via Lucana 150
75100 MATERA

Mme Marie-Noelle MICHAELIS

Interprète du Conseil de l'Europe
Via B. Latini 87
51033 FIRENZE

Mme Ana KACIC-ROSSETTI

Interprète du Conseil de l'Europe
Via Monte Fumarolo 48
06141 PONTE FELCINO (PG)

Mme Irma SANTI

Interprète du Conseil de l'Europe
Via Il Prato
50123 FIRENZE

Mme Anne WORONTZOFF

Interprète du Conseil de l'Europe
Via Goito 19
50133 FIRENZE

****

Sales agents for publications of the Council of Europe
Agents de vente des publications du Conseil de l'Europe

AUSTRALIA/AUSTRALIE
Hunter publications, 58A, Gipps Street
AUS-3066 COLLINGWOOD, Victoria
Fax: (61) 33 9 419 7154
E-mail: jpdavies@ozemail.com.au

AUSTRIA/AUTRICHE
Gerold und Co., Graben 31
A-1011 WIEN 1
Fax: (43) 1512 47 31 29
E-mail: buch@gerold.telecom.at

BELGIUM/BELGIQUE
La Librairie européenne SA
50, avenue A. Jonnart
B-1200 BRUXELLES 20
Fax: (32) 27 35 08 60
E-mail: info@libeurop.be

Jean de Lannoy
202, avenue du Roi
B-1060 BRUXELLES
Fax: (32) 25 38 08 41

CANADA
Renouf Publishing Company Limited
5369 Chemin Canotek Road
CDN-OTTAWA, Ontario, K1J 9J3
Fax: (1) 613 745 76 60

CZECH REPUBLIC/RÉPUBLIQUE TCHÈQUE
USIS, Publication Service
Havelkova 22
CZ-130 00 Praha 3
Fax: (420) 2 242 21 484

DENMARK/DANEMARK
Munksgaard
PO Box 2148
DK-1016 KØBENHAVN K
Fax: (45) 33 12 93 87

FINLAND/FINLANDE
Akateeminen Kirjakauppa
Keskuskatu 1, PO Box 218
SF-00381 HELSINKI
Fax: (358) 9 121 44 50
E-mail: akatilaus@stockmann.fi

GERMANY/ALLEMAGNE
UNO Verlag
Proppelsdorfer Allee 55
D-53115 BONN
Fax: (49) 228 21 74 92
E-mail: unoverlag@aol.com

GREECE/GRÈCE
Librairie Kauffmann
Mavrokordatou 9, GR-ATHINAI 106 78
Fax: (30) 13 23 03 20

HUNGARY/HONGRIE
Euro Info Service
Magyarország
Margitsziget (Európa Ház),
H-1138 BUDAPEST
Fax: (361) 302 50 35
E-mail: euroinfo@mail.matav.hu

IRELAND/IRLANDE
Government Stationery Office
4-5 Harcourt Road, IRL-DUBLIN 2
Fax: (353) 14 75 27 60

ISRAEL/ISRAËL
ROY International
41 Mishmar Hayarden Street
PO Box 13056
IL-69865 TEL AVIV
Fax: (972) 3 6499469
E-mail: royil@netvision.net.il

ITALY/ITALIE
Libreria Commissionaria Sansoni
Via Duca di Calabria, 1/1
Casella Postale 552, I-50125 FIRENZE
Fax: (39) 0 55 64 12 57

MALTA/MALTE
L. Sapienza & Sons Ltd
26 Republic Street
PO Box 36
VALLETTA CMR 01
Fax: (356) 233 621

NETHERLANDS/PAYS-BAS
De Lindeboom Internationale Publikaties b.v.
PO Box 202
NL-7480 AE HAAKSBERGEN
Fax: (31) 53 572 92 96

NORWAY/NORVÈGE
Akademika, A/S Universitetsbokhandel
PO Box 84, Blindern
N-0314 OSLO
Fax: (47) 22 85 30 53

POLAND/POLOGNE
Głowna Księgarnia Naukowa im. B. Prusa
Krakowskie Przedmiescie 7
PL-00-068 WARSZAWA
Fax: (48) 22 26 64 49

PORTUGAL
Livraria Portugal
Rua do Carmo, 70
P-1200 LISBOA
Fax: (351) 13 47 02 64

SPAIN/ESPAGNE
Mundi-Prensa Libros SA
Castelló 37, E-28001 MADRID
Fax: (34) 915 75 39 98
E-mail: libreria@mundiprensa.es

SWITZERLAND/SUISSE
Buchhandlung Heinimann & Co.
Kirchgasse 17, CH-8001 ZÜRICH
Fax: (41) 12 51 14 81

BERSY
Route d'Uvrier 15
CH-1958 LIVRIER/SION
Fax: (41) 27 203 73 32

UNITED KINGDOM/ROYAUME-UNI
TSO (formerly HMSO)
51 Nine Elms Lane
GB-LONDON SW8 5DR
Fax: (44) 171 873 82 00
E-mail: denise.perkins@theso.co.uk

UNITED STATES and CANADA/
ÉTATS-UNIS et CANADA
Manhattan Publishing Company
468 Albany Post Road
PO Box 850
CROTON-ON-HUDSON, NY 10520, USA
Fax: (1) 914 271 58 56
E-mail: Info@manhattanpublishing.com

STRASBOURG
Librairie Kléber
Palais de l'Europe
F-67075 STRASBOURG Cedex
Fax: +33 (0)3 88 52 91 21

Council of Europe Publishing/Editions du Conseil de l'Europe
Council of Europe/Conseil de l'Europe
F-67075 Strasbourg Cedex
Tel. +33 (0)3 88 41 25 81 – Fax +33 (0)3 88 41 39 10 – E-mail: publishing@coe.fr – Website: http://book.coe.fr

The

Yearning
Heart

Poems of Contemplation and Stillness

Hilary K Sinclair

ISBN: 978-1-64970-041-4 (Ebook)
        978-1-64970-042-1 (Softcover)

Contents

Poems with a Christian Connection

Refract the Lens of Time

Haiku

Preface

It has taken me many years before I even thought about publishing this small collection of poems. But now, upon re-reading them I feel they may speak to people, whose spirits may be lifted by sharing in these very private yet also universal experiences. Certainly when I read them again recently I felt an astonishing kinship with them, as they spoke to me afresh from the great unknown. I have consequently left most to speak for themselves without embellishment, only adding a historical comment where this illuminates the background of a poem, perhaps adding an explanatory context to it.

These poems compress eternal consciousness truths into a cauldron of mystic understanding where every phrase and word carries us into another dimension. The reader is asked to intuit meaning spontaneously while at the same time unpacking a cogent realisation of what the poem is saying. There is an underlying tautness in each line, challenging the reader to go deeper.

If anyone would like to contact me, my email address is:

sinclair.hk@gmail.com

Dedication

I dedicate these poems to the memory of my English teacher, Kathleen Flint, who fifty years ago introduced me to Emily Bronte, John Keats, Simone Weil, and a realm of mystical inspiration which began my still very incomplete journey. Also in grateful thanks to Rev David Bick, whose profound wisdom and reliable witness sustained me through many turbulent years. A few of these poems were written in the warm and friendly atmosphere of Wotton -under-Edge writers' group, helping me with inspiration and discipline.

I have appended an afterword for some of these poems, giving a little background to their creation. Others came 'out of the blue'.

Acknowledgments

I am thankful for the continuing work of the Clinical Theology Association, founded by Frank Lake in the sixties, and now called The Bridge Pastoral Foundation. Their ground breaking work in re-experiencing birth and neonatal trauma was pivotal for me. (www.bridgepastoralfoundation.org.uk)

Also for the regression work so brilliantly orchestrated by Simon Myerson in a group setting. (Previously of the Tavistock Clinic)

Many thanks to Pixabay, a brilliant copyright free photo archive, from where I sourced most of the photos accompanying these poems. Pixabay can be found at www.Pixabay.com

Introduction

I want to say thank you here for the people who have guided me on my journey in so many different ways. They are always with me in the underground of my senses informing me and comforting me. I think they formed my poetic imagination in ways I didn't know and wasn't aware of. I know that many readers will be familiar with these poems, and I mention them to flesh out some of their deep influences on me.

John Keats (English poet: born 1795—died 1821), has been dear to my heart for many years. He famously wrote "if poetry comes not as naturally as leaves on the tree it had better not come at all." I remember sitting waiting for a poem to arrive, and never forcing it. I think this is why I have written so few! Keats wrote to his friend, " Axioms of philosophy are not axioms unless they are proved upon our pulses." Meaning that you need to walk the talk. Contemplation is nothing without action.

"The problems of the world cannot possibly be solved by skeptics or cynics whose horizons are limited by the obvious realities. We need men who can dream of things that never were."

"My imagination is a monastery and I am its monk. I am certain of nothing but the holiness of the heart's affections, and the truth of imagination. Whatever the imagination seizes as Beauty must be truth -whether it existed before or not."

"Do you not see how necessary a world of pains and troubles is to school an intelligence and make it a soul?"
— John Keats, Letters of John Keats

At a high octane spiritual event in 1976, I 'met' the spirit of John Keats under a tree. Such a fleeting yet intense moment:

"The Autumn leaves lie damp upon the ground I sift them through and try to rake them up Golden they flitter softly through my fingers Falling gently into the soft mud. Then a voice is heard. Deep and insistent it calls to me 'John, John' I cry out and run forward to make this moment mine. I fully expect him to run out from under the tree. But he does not. Lost in infinity, a victim of history."

Emily Bronte
When I was 16 I went all the way to Haworth in Yorkshire to visit the moors and landscape inhabited by the Brontë sisters. I am so thankful and amazed that my parents allowed me to go by train all on my own in 1957. I had a very strong connection to Emily Brontë and her poetry. She wrote the famous poem "No Coward Soul is Mine" which is an in inexpressibly deep understanding of higher consciousness. She wrote several other mystical poems including "The Prisoner" with its famous description of contemplative ecstasy. My english teacher introduced me to all these poems, and I am so thankful for that.

Gerard Manley Hopkins

This enigmatic poet has a unique poetic style with a quality of profundity expressed in idiosyncratic lyrical verse.

Three favourite poems are:

"No worst, there is none. Pitched past pitch of grief... O the mind, mind has mountains; cliffs of falls Frightful, sheer, no-man-fathomed. Hold them cheap May who ne'er hung there."

God's Grandeur

"The world is charged with the grandeur of God. It will flame out, like shining from shook foil; "

Peace

"When will you ever, Peace, wild wooddove, shy wings shut, Your round me roaming end, and under be my boughs?"

Simone Weil: French philosopher and mystic (died 1943) I also first encountered Simone Weil in my six form years.

Her essays in Waiting on God called Reflections on the Right use of School Studies, and Forms of the Implicit Love of God, had a profound influence on me, as she speaks of the crucial importance of attention, necessity and free will, and the piercing of the veil, to apprehend God.Her work has often been misunderstood and misinterpreted but I think it's about an ineluctable sense of the divine.

In conclusion, I dare to hope that some of my poems may, as Keats said about poetry, "strike the reader as a wording of his own highest thoughts and seem almost a remembrance"

O clear the mind

Let it be blank

A white sheet, blank parchment,

Curl, uncurl softly.

No to lethargy – tranquillity –

How to fight the one and achieve the other.

New Grace

New grace, new space, new year

Make a place, make a place.

What is unknown will softly unfold

In the womb of time.

Truth is always only now-

The eternal moment, pure and

Without blemish,

Surrender to it, and be glad

© Hilary Sinclair 1976

Galaxies

The superstructure of the galaxies is modelled in man's mind

His interwoven consciousness among the stars.

"Looking through a glass onion"*

-not peeled, but shattered painfully,

The pathway to the soul is resonant with life.

*Lennon/ McCartney quote.

Time Tunnel

I am long drawn out into the tunnel of time;

Aimlessly wandering through uncharted darkness,

infusing a soft sad glow,

growing incandescent with pain.

Perhaps one day I'll return to my own centre and know the truth.

The hollow core of loneliness is universal,

The remedy only is uniquely loving.

Enlightenment Intensive

I have trodden in the vacant interstellar spaces

I have frozen in the hub of the universe

The sound of stillness is in my soul.

I have heard the silence of a hawthorn tree

I have felt the trembling cracking of its branches

I know its strength and its fragility.

I have seen hope and love shine from another's face

I have been transfixed by love, and felt another's doubting agony

I have met another across infinite space.

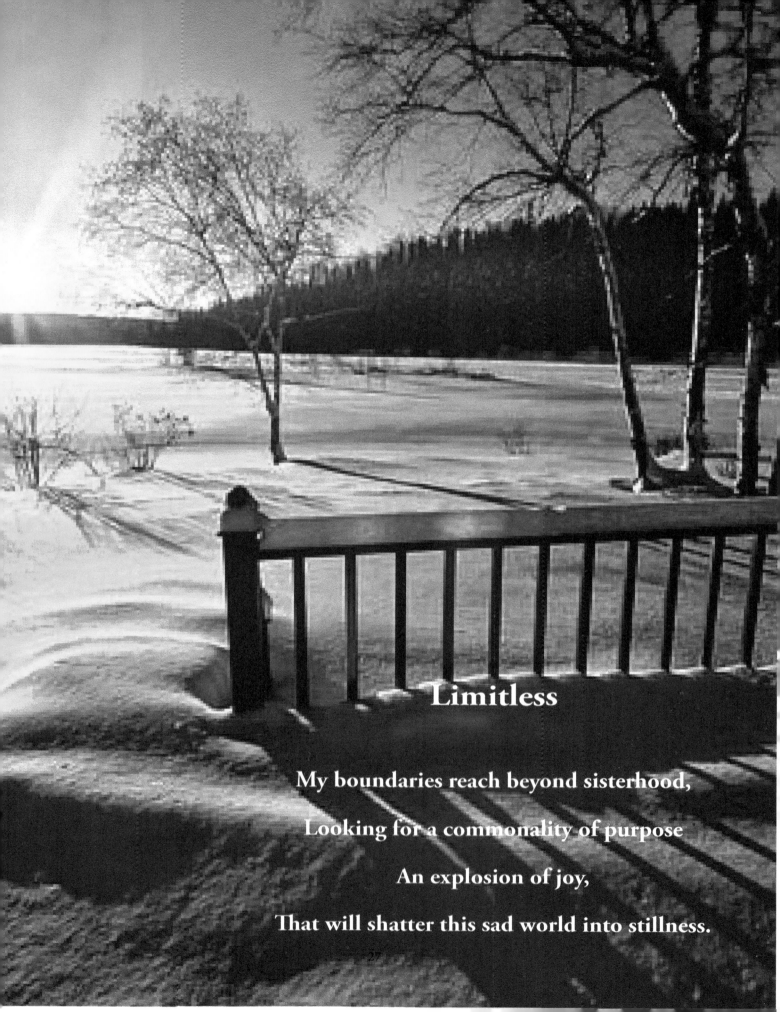

Limitless

My boundaries reach beyond sisterhood,

Looking for a commonality of purpose

An explosion of joy,

That will shatter this sad world into stillness.

Spring

The crocus cracks the cold unforgiving ground

Its spike spears the implacable earth

While yellow daffodils yawn at the pale sun.

Torrents tumble over the stone overhang

Plunging into the clear pool.

White mist rises, a silent cloud,

Witness to a wet Spring

And the falling rain.

Soon summer blossoms melt our hardened hearts

And blooms assail our heightened sense

With fragrances of long ago.

30

Butterflies

Summer ends suddenly, butterflies all gone,

beautiful wings collapsed into dusky husks

dewlit grass, calm and clear

But what of the lonely, the old ones

querulously hunched over twilight fires,

Like the butterflies they too will have their end.

Countryside

The cerulean canopy arches over the quiet landscape,

Tall larches leap, reaching upwards to the sky,

The trees trickling down a faint summer's sun.

Green glowing grass comforts a chubby rabbit, surprised eyes

inquisitively roving.

In gathering dew, smaller still, the slugs uncurl,

Intent on their evening roaming.

The river ferments under the ancient stone bridge

The throaty bleat of a distant sheep seizes the still air.

The harmony of England at rest folds us in thrall.

34

Déjà vu

A pattern in time

Twice repeated.

Seeing the leaf fall again.

Sudden energy bursts between two poles,

This has happened before, we think;

A split second divides present from past,

And merges it again.

Falling

The shackles clicked, quick as a flash

The neat nylon pink and blue ropes flickered like demented butterflies

Bounced, bounded, streamed through the cleats,

Plunging down the face of the rock

Taking me with them.

The world spun sideways,

My body shuddered, cavorting in empty space.

Abruptly, explosively, the belays took the strain

Holding the rope taut.

My safety.

The view was amazing.

Grenze

Yellow, red and black,

Each post stands in the land,

Stands proud before an industrial strength fence:

Tall sentinels of alien pain.

A nation enslaved,

Trenchant history in time remembered

Soldiering on through lost campaigns:

The unsuccessful conclusion of a failed experiment.

A swathe of churned up earth morphs into the distant mist

And on the sentry towers

Embittered soldiers loll with vacant eyes.

Oil

The scowling cloud erupts, acrid portent from the burning sand

Noxious, routinely black smoke rises where the

Oil gushes gashes from a parched earth

Implicating us in its frenzied quest for fodder.

Seagulls squawk with raucous fervour

Ignorant of imminent death

Nelson

Ships nestle like flies

Cradled on the sun-splashed water

Canon cock their muzzles, their black throats afire

Suddenly a canon roars, a musket flashes

Nelson hits the deck

The memory is etched, frozen in time

The image of a dying man

And the monumental churning of the sea.

Christmas

Christmas

Is not to conceptualise a meaning, rather know a truth,

Continuity of friendship,

Superficiality of contact,

Just nodding acquaintance,

Making up for lost time.

Christmas

Is sharing the joy of children,

Forgetting frustration,

Looking for a meaning;

Life is extreme in its demands.

Christmas

Clockwork roundabout of the seasons,

Rebelling against cotton wool Father Christmases

And bloated plastic clowns.

The sugar coated bitter pill of another year gone.

Accepting what is.

Kaleidoscope

The rhythm grows

The pattern falls

One man's meat

Is another man's poison.

To each his own reality

Yet we would like it to be absolute

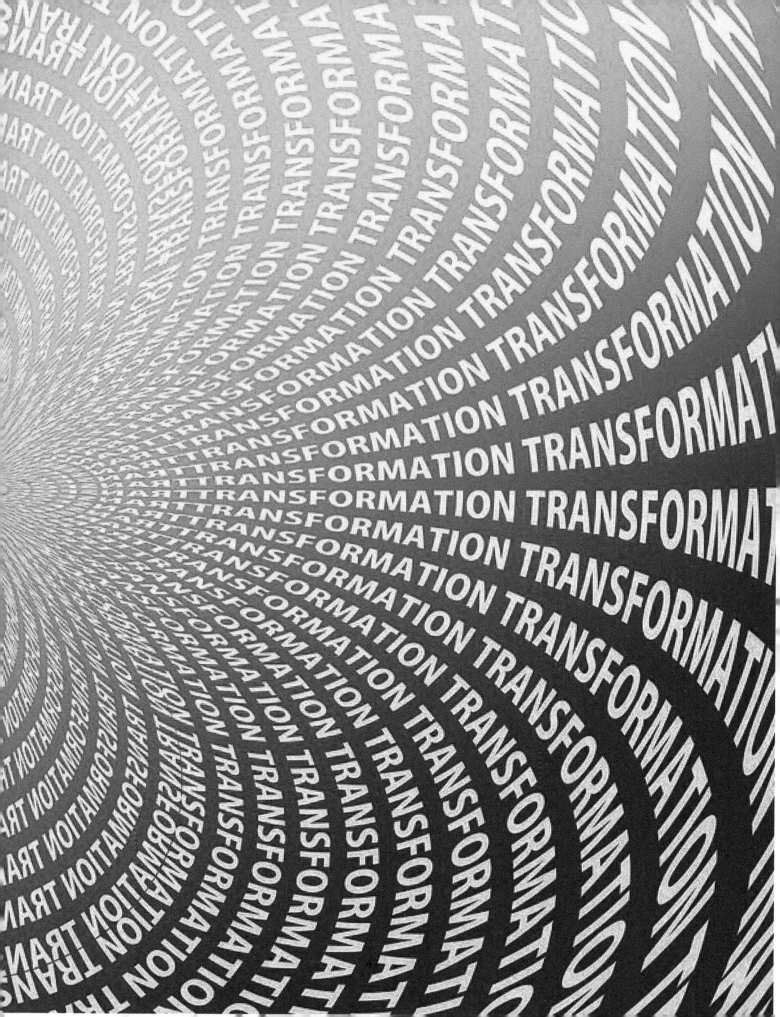

Floating, Singing

Not the message, not the context,

But the pure voice of pain.

Out of the hurting, haunting void

Hurtles the sound of being,

Floating, singing,

The echo of a more satisfactory world.

Poems with a
Christian Connection

Beginnings

No beginning, no end; so says the Tao,

But I believe in one point in created time when the world began.

At least I think I do.

Why is a point more scrupulous than an aeon?

Everything has a beginning; but does it have an end?

My beginning was at conception, or was it before?

A network of genetic formulae links me to the first man.

"As in Adam all die, so in Christ all are made alive."

"Before Abraham was, I AM"

The shout of Jesus echoes down the years:

A panegyric to time.

Sitting on the sea wall steps at Weymouth

No personal sorrow, mine,

Only the frustrate sickness of humanity,

Seeking yet in sin to save its dying soul.

The throbbing of the sea dispassionate

Throws on the cold stone steps

Salt tears of gleaming dew,

Lit by the golden bars of the late sun.

The wide white waves wash in tinged with fire

But we are blind to see and sun.

God only can inspire.

If there is no hope in man, and we alive

God must protect us or our life is death.

Hovering

Is there anywhere else

Hovering far over me to hide ?

Sick with a glut of words-faint attempts to tie you up

into something I can understand.

Loving you-wanting to communicate you

-your wisdom-your peace, your joy-

When I don't possess it-only guess at it-is that a sin?

Catch me in time before I fall.

I am not ready to make the journey on my own.

So few gone ahead-so many behind, the enemy sneers

And where are those who are with me on the way?

I need them-I need to hold their hand in an abandoned leap-

And yet a measured walk into the unknown chasm of your vast emptiness.

Eagles Wings

Help me to fly, serene on eagle's wings

Secure within the trust that your love brings.

Help me to soar in faith to your eternal throne

Bearing the burdens of your love in every victory won.

Early poem 1977-8

Holy Spirit thank you

For gestalting me.

Indeed you form, inform and move me

Now I know

You own no other name.

Easter Morning

Transported through time,

On the edge of the future I stand

Teetering on the brink of a new beginning.

Eternity stretches behind and before.

The bird of light lifts wings of wonder,

Soaring into the still air.

Go with him

for he will not land again.

PINK ROSES

PINK ROSES out of heavenly ardour blown

Blossoming from the humid earth;

What bright dewdrops reflect your holy face

And falling, mingle with the grass fresh mown.

(We know you're on the case.)

A promise of perfumed petals sown,

Brings a blush of profusion

A swell of lush confusion, comforting strained muscles in my heart.

In this soft stream of being my senses re-orient,

reform and poise themselves for truth.

Why can't truth be gentle like the roses?

Seawall at Othona

Stately white sails in gracious procession, far out in the estuary-

Beyond - the thin dark horizon, the bright blue sea.

Nearer, the obscurity of the mudflats

- the outward march of serried staves,

Marshalling the sand.

Eleven black barges silently guard the foreshore,

Sturdy barriers to the incoming tide;

The encroaching sand silts there,

warding off the power of the North Sea.

But the power of the silence is more commanding;

No sound of crashing wave

But only the soft blowing of the wind

Lifting us into the comfort of God

Epitaph of an Enneagram "One"

Focusing on the One who is All

Not on the chaotic nightmare of the deep,

Surrounded by a pure circle of what is—

This could be bliss.

How to still the concatenating murmurs of disquiet

The frenzy of assessment, computation by the hour,

A summation of chaos which seizes

Constricts and narrows life.

Yes, my perfection, that for which I yearn,

Draws me steadfastly forward.

But the drawing out of the silent pool

Is hard to come by,

Existing only in a

Small piece of bread.

Holy Spirit

With trembling expectation

We await your fiery perturbation Upturning our

compliant rituals, our dusty, devious routines.

Surprise us with your surge of white hot truth,

Clear bell of innocence, shining star of integrity.

Immerse us in a swelling ocean of peace, an

activity of consciousness Propelling us richly

onward into the tapestry of our separate futures.

Our separateness will become one day a fusion

and union of eternal fruitfulness.

Refract the Lens of Time

Mayhem's Gate: Post 9/11

Refract the lens of time.

Hush into stillness the sun of centuries.

Too many memories lie verdant;-

the crimson gash of warring faiths

each swallowed by the dark maw, traitors' gate.

Those who believe the power is theirs

Theirs the ultimate of right

Must ride forever on its aching cusp.

Theirs the false belief, proclaimed as truth

Opening wide the gate to mayhem.

At Tyburn, Oxford, York, the Tower

The martyrs' blood still flows unceasingly-

That red bloom is the flower

That speaks of dogma's inhumanity.

It is a monstrous paradox

That any sound religion

Should turn itself upon its head

And exact an unforgiving retribution.

The sinews of hatred vibrate in a symphony of apocalyptic expectation.

The horsemen of Western capitalism

Ride roughshod across the plain.

Too late, too late the lament for latter day satanic mills

And for sharing our plunder with the poor.

Mayhem's Gate

Those who believe the power is theirs,

Theirs the ultimate of right,

Must ride forever on its aching cusp.

Theirs the false belief, proclaimed as truth

Opening wide the gate to mayhem.

"You have heard that it was said,

'Eye for eye and tooth for tooth'.

But I tell you, do not resist an evil person.

If someone strikes you on the right cheek, turn to him the other also."

And now we walk as in a mist of unseen hfear

Fleeing the ghost of our own shadow selves,

Reluctantly embracing a world of inconstant uncertainty,

We brace ourselves for disaster.

"Find rest, O my soul, in God alone; my help comes from him."

Those who believe the power is theirs,

Theirs the ultimate of right,

Must ride forever on its aching cusp.

Theirs the false belief, proclaimed as truth

Opening wide the gate to Mayhem.

Furnace

From the furnace of pure gold

Flames ascend to the blue sky –

White hot the truth

that burns into the heart of man –

brings fruit that ripens on the tree,

On the tree of Calvary

Brass Ceiling

The brass ceiling,

The impenetrable sky,

The leaden atmosphere,

All are sealing me off from the inflowing presence of God.

Where is the shaft of light spearing the darkness,

Swelling, possessing the black chasm of fear,

Rendering it impotent?

I look inside,

The rough fabric is scarred, clotted with blood.

(An angel speaks:)

"It is not bright raiment we look for,

but a robe that envelops the great wound of the world,

A wound that pricks out lies and obfuscations,

secret malice and murderous intent,

that makes criminals, not martyrs, of us all."

Oh, but this is too much, too dramatic by far.

We would prefer to retire to our quiet firesides by the telly and sip our

Ovaltine in peace.

Don't speak of war and rumours of war.

But we cannot abort the process of destruction on our own;

we must live through it, embrace it and savour it.

How else can we find Him who is our peace.

(Finally, Our Lord says this:)

Can you drink the cup which I drink and share the bread I give?

What will you surrender to the coming King?

Love's Longing

19th April 1990

Beyond the longing of my love

There is emptiness.

A space apart for

Him to fill.

Haiku

Haiku

Just one haiku shines

A jewel glittering darkly

Glows eternally

Concisely speaking

It encapsulates the thought

Transcending spirit

Wind soughing gently

Coaxing brown leaves to fall

Leaving the tree bare

Unfurling white snail

Delicately slithering

Moves gently away

Struggle

Another day gone

The end is never in sight

What a fiasco

Covid this Easter

Threatening all we hold dear

We will rise again

Death stalking the land

Keeping head above water

Welcome now Spirit

Ego muscles in

Supplanting higher wisdom

I long to break through

Ego driven world

Constantly eroding life

Pray for these people

Small self carries on

Infiltrating my soul path

So hampering me

Where is my heart's core

Shrivellled up like a dry prune

Emotion floods in

Harmony

Where is the focus
Shining a heavenly light
The gateway of truth?

One jot and tittle
Snap shot of recorded time
Never repeated

Above and below
Pinpointed in the balance
Straddling awareness

Held in vibration
Now transcending the ego
Unspeakable peace

Heart opening now
So quietly, stealthily
Abundance awaits

Secret well within

Awakening the glory

Universal love

All beneficent

An ocean of beingness

Utter paradox

O intricate web

Encapsulating all life

For ever awake

Fullness of quiet peace

My monkey mind is now still

Bathing in the light

Beyond my ego

In the transparent moment

There is nothingness

Transcending ego

Silent realms beyond thinking

Coming home at last

End Notes

Enlightenment Intensive

The enlightenment intensive format, back in the seventies, enabled at that time some of the most stimulating, awareness producing, even mystical events in my life. This poem reflects that:

I once experienced the causal state of the Void during an Enlightenment Intensive in the seventies. I have never forgotten it. There was complete nothingness: emptiness. No stars or galaxies. Just nothing. But not frightening. Comfortable. Fulness in a vacuum.

Apparently, this state is quite frequently experienced by participants in an EI.

I now realise that this was ultimate conscious awareness. It was not 'I' that was experiencing this. For a brief moment 'I' was not there. It was only the consciousness.

Butterflies

I wrote this poem after coming home from taking my daughter to Primary School for her first day at school. I Suddenly became aware of the finiteness of life.

Grenze

This was written in Duderstadt on an official visit with Stroud District Council, when we visited the frontier between East and West Germany. Two villages separated from each other by no man's land.

Nelson

A poem written in 2005 as part of the commemoration of the battle of Trafalgar.

Sea at Weymouth

I wrote this at the age of 17, full of teenage angst.

Easter Morning

Written during the celebration of the Easter triduum led by Jim Cotter at Othona, Burton Bradstock

Sea Wall at Othona

Written on the sea wall of the Othona community at Bradwell on Sea, Essex

Epitaph for an Enneagram 'One'

Written during an Enneagram workshop at Emmaus House, Bristol.

About the Author

Hilary Sinclair is a qualified spiritual director and graduate teacher (long since retired) She originally worked in the field of psychodynamic and group psychotherapy and graduated from the University of Cambridge in the UK. During her post graduate education studies at Bristol University an ongoing experience in a leaderless group referencing the work of WR Bion, first sparked her interest in psychodynamic psychology and social interaction.

She has always loved poetry, including works by Kathleen Raine, Emily Bronte, Gerard Manley Hopkins and John Keats. Her 'mystic' consciousness was first triggered as a teenager, by reading Simone Weil: Waiting on God

Exposure to intense spiritual pressure in a fundamentalist Christian Fellowship contributed to a severe mental breakdown in the eighties, which opened the gates to a more tranquil and contemplative life, where she derived much solace and inspiration from the works of St John of the Cross. Discovering Ken Wllber's Integral (AQUAL) world view led to an unexpected expanded consciousness which gave her the courage to publish this small volume of poems